T0198613

FAILS TO MEET EXPECTATIONS

Performance Review Strategies for
Underperforming Employees

Corey Sandler and Janice Keefe

Adams Media
New York   London   Toronto   Sydney   New Delhi

Adams Media
An Imprint of Simon & Schuster, Inc.
57 Littlefield Street
Avon, Massachusetts 02322

Copyright © 2008 by Word Association, Inc.

For information about special discounts for bulk purchases, please
contact Simon & Schuster Special Sales at 1-866-506-1949 or
business@simonandschuster.com.

The Simon & Schuster Speakers Bureau can bring authors to your
live event. For more information or to book an event contact the
Simon & Schuster Speakers Bureau at 1-866-248-3049 or visit
our website at www.simonspeakers.com.

Manufactured in the United States of America

10 9 8 7 6 5 4 3 2 1

Library of Congress Cataloging-in-Publication Data has been
applied for.

ISBN 978-1-59869-145-0

Acknowledgments

We thank our publishing partners at Adams Media, including Gary Krebs, Andrea Norville, Peter Archer, Virginia Beck, and Catherine Forrest Getzie.

Thanks, too, to Ed Claflin for helping extend the series to another chapter.

And finally, thanks to you, the reader. We know that you have purchased this book because you have a job to accomplish. We hope we receive high scores on your evaluation in the field.

CONTENTS

Introduction

THE NEED TO MEET EXPECTATIONS

VERY FEW OF US enjoy making threats, and even fewer of us take pleasure in carrying them through. Yet that is the basis of the employer-employee or manager-subordinate relationship: If you want to hold on to your job or your title, you'll have to do what we ask of you and do it well.

In general, unless there is an employment contract or a collective-bargaining agreement or another form of promise in effect, all employees work on an "at-will" basis. That means the employer can choose to dismiss someone for a good reason or for no reason at all. Where the danger lies is this: dismissing someone for a bad reason.

Most of us have found various ways to deal with situations in which a continued relationship is paramount. We do this in a family with our children or spouse or significant other. We seek ways to gently or firmly nudge someone we respect to act in a more healthy or productive way.

When it comes to the workplace, the bottom line is . . . well, the bottom line. In most cases, an organization has a substantial investment in training, salary already paid, benefits accrued, and the accumulated experience of its employees.

Unless there has been a serious violation of a core value of the company (or a credible accusation or conviction of a crime), it makes sense to try to rehabilitate a worker who is underperforming or otherwise not meeting expectations.

Not every employee can or should be kept on the payroll at any cost. But the purpose of this book is to help managers find the words and phrases to use in verbal and written communication with employees who are failing to meet expectations.

We'll present cases in an escalating ladder of messages:

- A verbal notification of concern
- A memo to file that documents the conversation, including any responses made by the employee. The memo also notes any directions given to the employee, as well as any requests made to other managers.
- A memo to file that records the details of any offer of assistance made to the employee, including training, special consulting, or adaptations to the job description or the way in which the job is to be performed
- An element of a performance evaluation acknowledging progress made on the issue in contention
- An alternate version of a performance evaluation putting on the record a continuing or renewed failure to meet expectations
- A written warning requiring a change in behavior or performance or a notification of intent to reassign or terminate employment

The last chapter of this book includes an interview with a well-respected attorney who is an authority on employment laws and issues. Our discussion touches on general procedures for managers dealing with personnel as well as hot-button legal issues.

A WORD *to the* WISE

As with every other element of this book, please bear this warning in mind: If you have any concern about a possible violation of law or regulations by an employee or any worries that you may be drawn into a lawsuit or other legal action, stop! Contact your human resources department or go directly to your in-house attorney or outside counsel. A quick phone call could save a huge amount of time, effort, and money. The same goes for drafting an employee handbook. This is a task for a trained human resources professional and one that often also involves approval by an attorney.

Our goal in this book is to give you the tools to write your own memos and performance evaluations within the framework developed by your human resources department or an attorney. Each of the memos and evaluation fragments included in this book is intended for you to use or adapt in your own work. This book is copyrighted, which means you are not allowed to photocopy, scan, or otherwise reproduce it as a whole product. However, you are welcome to adapt any of the memos and evaluations to your own needs as a manager.

The Employee Evaluation Framework

We're gathered in writing and reading this book because we believe the proper way to deal with an employee who fails to meet expectations is to follow a straightforward, honest, and fair process that is consistently applied to all members of staff. In many situations, the course of action is encompassed within the employee evaluation process.

Your organization should have a detailed, written description of the procedure and expectations included in an evaluation; it's an essential part of a plan for success for everyone involved.

Ratings Tools

Some companies, organizations, and agencies use a very general written evaluation that allows for a great deal of customization to the needs of the employee and the manager, and the nature of work performed. The disadvantage of this style is the danger that a manager will commit to writing something that could be challenged in court or other legal proceeding.

Other organizations use a numerical scale that rates employees from 1 to 10. This system expresses variations that might go from "fails to meet expectations" to "superlative in every aspect." Though it requires more work by the manager, a broader range of ratings (1 to 10 is much better than 1 to 5) allows more flexibility in marking problems and noting improvement.

A narrow scale can cause problems if an employee challenges a reassignment, disciplinary action, or termination. A judge or a jury or other fact-finder might not be willing to agree that an employee with an average score of 3.0 is that much different than one with ratings that average 4.1. On the other hand, the difference between a 3.0 and an 8.2 seems much more significant.

For the same reason, it is important that managers not try to always find something nice to say about an employee who is performing at levels lower than expected. If you are concentrating on documenting the fact that a worker is consistently missing deadlines or using sick days for vacation time (if that is prohibited in your employee manual), don't confuse the issue by including in the employee evaluation the fact that this same worker is "well-organized" and "a good team player."

We do, though, recommend that you draw the distinction between the person and his or her actions. There is nothing wrong (and in fact, it is a decent thing to do) to note that you "value Mr. Jones's efforts and hope for his success" at the same time as you put into writing your assessment that Mr. Jones "fails to meet our expectations in delivering reports on time and of acceptable quality."

This book concentrates on employees who are performing at less than acceptable levels. We also recommend that you consult *Performance Appraisals That Work* from Adams Media, written by the same authors who brought you the volume you are reading right now. For information, consult *www.adamsmedia.com* or *www.econo guide.com.* In this section, we'll recap some of the most important elements of performance appraisals, as we presented them in *Performance Appraisals That Work.*

Be Prepared

Nothing you say in an employee evaluation session or a written personnel memo should come as a total surprise to the worker receiving the appraisal. If a staffer has had great success, he or she should already know of the organization's appreciation through regular interaction with supervisors and recipients of services. If an employee has been struggling, the supervisor or department head should have been involved at the earliest signs of trouble, gently and appropriately pointing out mistakes or inefficiencies and suggesting paths to improvement.

If you are about to deliver a less-than-favorable evaluation, that appraisal should be as specific as possible in five very important ways:

1. Reference should be made to the job description or other documents that lay out expectations of quality and quantity of work and that encompass the core values or mission statement of the organization. It is not fair—and it is a weak legal position—to make critical comments on job performance about an employee who has not been given a clear and specific job description. Similarly, a judgment of inadequate performance on tasks that are not in the job description is generally not supportable.

2. As a manager, you must take the time to be completely up to date on current assignments and accomplishments of the employee. If the staffer does not work directly for you, review the situation with his or her immediate supervisor.

3. Be specific about problems with productivity, quality of work, interactions with coworkers or clients, or any other problematic behavior or incidents that have taken place in the workplace or are directly related to the job. If there are any specific complaints from supervisors, coworkers, clients, or customers you should read them and conduct any necessary investigation to obtain full details and follow proper procedure regarding how they are handled in an employee evaluation.

4. Be as precise as possible. Stating in writing or orally that "Ms. Jones has not been doing such a great job lately" does not help the employee improve and does not establish a path toward dismissal or reassignment if that is eventually deemed necessary. Instead, a proper evaluation could declare, "Ms. Jones has fallen at least 10 percent below sales goals for three consecutive quarters," or "Ms. Jones was directed to oversee the establishment of a computer-tagged inventory process to be effective on or before January 1, and this was not accomplished."

5. Have a plan. Offer praise where it is justified—always a good way to start out on an evaluation—then offer specific suggestions on ways to improve performance. These can be as simple as direct coaching or goal setting, or it can involve a recommendation or assignment to basic or advanced training sessions.

A WORD *to the* WISE

If any of the matters involved in an employee evaluation appears to cross over to illegal behavior or to serious violations of the organization's policies, you should immediately involve the human resources department, the in-house attorney, or outside counsel. In the same vein, make sure you take care not to violate privacy rules and regulations, which apply to many areas including medical records and legal proceedings.

Be Fair

Sociologists, political scientists, and other specialists in human interactions talk about the importance of "transparency" in processes. This is what they mean. Unless there are legal reasons to act otherwise, make all your personnel and performance evaluations in the open—at least as far as the employee is concerned. Don't withhold information unnecessarily. Follow all the rules in the same manner for all employees performing the same sort of work.

An employee evaluation is not a place for you, as a supervisor, to indicate whether you like or dislike a person or object or approve of someone's personal attributes. Your task is to fairly and consistently judge whether the employee has done what has been asked of him or her and has met reasonable goals.

Judge only behavior and accomplishments and only those directly related to the job. To state what should be obvious to any employer or supervisor, a person's race, sex, sexual orientation, religion, politics, and personal beliefs are off-limits unless it can be shown that they materially affect a person's ability to perform a job. If one of these protected categories is involved in an evaluation, step back and get an employment lawyer involved before you say or do anything.

Goals and Standards

It is important to distinguish between goals and standards. A goal is a target, while a standard is a rule. An employee can be disciplined or dismissed for serious violations of either, providing the rules and standards are fairly defined and equitably applied.

Some goals can be quite specific and can be judged objectively—sales targets are either met or not met, for example. Other goals, such as quality of service, are by definition judged subjectively. The employee has to accept the goal as possible. Similarly, an employer has to either accept or reject an employee's stated goal as something that is appropriate to the organization and in keeping with its reasoned appraisal of the worker's abilities.

Standards can also be specific—for instance, violation of criminal or civil law is not acceptable behavior—or can require subjective judgments, such as whether an employee is properly representing the company. At many organizations, the employee handbook includes a code of conduct, a formal declaration that requires adherence to federal, state, and local laws, and a mission statement that lays out a corporate culture.

Ignorance of the contents of the job description or the employee handbook is not an acceptable excuse for failure to follow the rules. Indeed, a claim of ignorance of the organization's expectations can in and of itself be a reason for discipline or dismissal.

Be Reasonable

If your goal is to find a way to help an employee improve his or her performance and stay in the organization, as it should be, don't handicap the chances of success by setting unreasonable goals or establishing an impossible-to-achieve deadline. Not only is this unfair to the employee and unlikely to result in rehabilitation of someone in whom the organization has invested time and money, it also might result in increased legal exposure if a lawsuit is filed.

As a supervisor, you should not invite an employee to dispute your findings or otherwise engage in an argument. However, it is often very useful to engage the employee in determining how best to fix problems that have been identified in the employee evaluation. In doing so, the worker is subscribing to the effort to raise his or her performance to an acceptable level.

If the employee tells you that she cannot perform a particular task on the computer because she has not been properly trained, the solution—or at least a step toward a solution—is obvious. The evaluation should state that training should be arranged and that another evaluation will be performed after it has been accomplished.

If a staffer responds to a critique by a manager by saying that he needs special assistance to physically accomplish the job (a step-stool, a magnifying glass, or a custom tool, for example) the organization may consider this a reasonable accommodation of a valued employee. In fact, federal law may require reasonable efforts under the Americans with Disabilities Act or other statutes. There is nothing in the law that requires an employer to hire a blind truck driver or to keep an employee in a particular job if he or she becomes unable to perform the task; however, be sure to involve your human resources department, in-house attorney, or outside counsel in any decision based on physical or medical disability.

If the problem seems to be one of a personality or behavioral mismatch in the workplace—one that violates a clearly defined code of conduct or elements of the job description—it is appropriate to require the employee to attend individual or group training or counseling and to require follow-up evaluations to check on progress. Examples include anger management courses, anti-bias training, and courses dealing with other human resources concerns.

Be Flexible

Although as a manager it is essential that you maintain control of all employee evaluation proceedings, it is also important that you allow for the possibility that your assessment is incorrect or that the staffer can make a credible case for extenuating circumstances. Your employee might have some constructive ideas to improve his or her own job or general operations.

Does the employee make a credible case that he or she has not received sufficient training or support? Is there a conflict with another employee or department? Is it possible that the company or organizational procedures make it difficult or impossible to accomplish goals, or does the employee have good suggestions to improve operations?

There is also the possibility that an employee's personal situation has interfered with productivity or otherwise affected behavior. It is generally not proper to inquire about personal life or health. If an employee offers information that is relevant to his or her job situation, you may decide it is appropriate to listen. However, do not make any promises other than to consult with your human resources department or legal counsel. Make certain you do not disclose information that is required to be kept private. Your legal counsel may ask that the employee sign a release to permit discussion and possible actions related to protected personal information.

Feedback

The details of a performance appraisal are confidential, usually available only to the employee, direct supervisors, and the human resources department. Be specific in your positive feedback to an employee. (Aside from being politically incorrect, an "Atta boy" or an "Atta girl" comment has no substance.) Tell someone (or send a memo or e-mail), "Your suggestions on the new marketing campaign were right on target. I'll keep you up to date on any decisions we make in this area."

Combine positive comments with reference to previously identified issues. "I was pleased to see that you are making a real effort to immediately convey the results of your marketing research to the design department when you see a sales opportunity. Your suggestions for modification of the Super Genie were very well thought out. This was one of the areas we discussed in your performance evaluation in January, and this is very much what I hoped to see."

If what you see is not what you want, the proper procedure—which should be outlined in the employee manual—would be something like this: In a discrete manner that would not cause embarrassment, ask the employee to attend a meeting or send an e-mail or memo requesting the same.

In the privacy of an office or closed-door conference room, explain that you want to discuss a matter of performance or an issue related to an element of the job description or the employee manual. Maintain a calm and professional manner, use your memos as the basis of what you say, and take careful notes on any responses by the employee.

If you have any concerns about the behavior of the employee or if you believe there is the possibility of a legal action, inform the human resources department or in-house or outside counsel in advance. They may suggest strategies or ask to be in attendance.

You're Fired

Sometimes there's nothing left to do but prepare an exit strategy. Like it or not, in many cases this represents a failure on both sides of the equation. Someone may have been given a job despite being not qualified or capable of fulfilling its requirements. Someone may have needed some extra training that was not available or not appropriate to his or her abilities or background.

There are, of course, also situations in which the employee has simply acted in an unacceptable manner. These are the sort of thresholds that are spelled out in the employee manual, a code of conduct, or the job description. They include certain arrests or convictions or violations of civil laws or regulations that take place outside of the workplace as well as improper conduct that takes place at the job. Once again, the key is for the rules to be applied equally to all members of a class of workers. You will likely open your organization to increased exposure if two employees commit the same or substantially similar offenses and one is dismissed while the other is allowed to stay on the payroll.

Then there are qualitative judgments. An employer is allowed to dismiss an employee who, though given all appropriate training and guidance, proves unable to produce work of an acceptable quality or is unable to interact with other employees. Again, any such judgment has to be equitably applied to all staffers. Some employment-law attorneys will counsel that the organization's employee manual and the job description include an initial probationary period after hiring during which a worker's status is considered something short of permanent. This is intended to put new employees on notice that they have to prove they are capable of performing the job.

With all these safeguards in place, if the decision is made to terminate an employee, the supervisor or manager should be able to consult—and should follow step-by-step—a process established by the organization's human resources department and approved by in-house or outside counsel. There may be forms and reports to be filled out and approved; there may be a requirement for advance notification to the human resources department; and there almost certainly will be an insistence on documentation of every step in the hiring, employee evaluation, and dismissal process.

Chapter 1

ABSENTEEISM AND TARDINESS

AT THE HEART of the hiring process is an agreement—a form of contract—that the new employee will show up and perform the job when he or she is needed and expected. The employer has the right to depend on an employee to fulfill the terms of that contract.

A job may come with a rigid, set schedule: Monday to Friday from 9 A.M. to 5 P.M. with half an hour off for lunch, for example. Or the job may be one in which the schedule changes from week to week or month to month, with workers given advance notice of the days and hours they are due to be at their jobs.

In either case, the essence of the deal is this: Within the agreed-upon framework, the employee promises to accept and follow a schedule assigned by the employer.

If the working hours or absenteeism policy for a particular unit differs in any way from other units in the organization, the difference should be laid out in writing. For example, maintenance or emergency response employees may be on call for certain hours or days of the week even if they are not required to be at work. The policy should explain how they are rewarded—with extra pay, compensatory time off, or both—if they are summoned.

Although employers are generally given leeway to make adjustments in working hours or days—as long as changes are equitable and not discriminatory—consult with your human resources office or in-house attorney before making changes to pre-established organizational policies.

A WORD to the WISE

It is always to your benefit as an employer or supervisor to begin the relationship with a new employee—or a staffer who is transferred or promoted into a new unit—by going over a written set of expectations and rules of conduct. That's the beauty of having an employee manual.

Excused Absences

Any permanent job and many part-time or temporary jobs provide a specified amount of sick time, personal days, holidays, vacations, and other packages of paid or unpaid time off. As with all of the examples given in this book, there is a major distinction between the rights of the employer (and the employee) when a worker is considered a "casual" or part-time hourly worker as opposed to someone who is "permanent" or otherwise on the payrolls of the employer.

Classes of Workers

Consult with your human resources office or in-house attorney if you do not understand your organization's differentiation of workers into various classes. You may be dealing with permanent employees, temporary employees, at-will workers, contract workers, consultants, casual workers, or another of dozens of labor terms.

In general, the full set of company policies, procedures, and benefits are usually aimed at permanent employees. Temporary or at-will employees can usually be terminated or reassigned (if they choose to accept a different position) at any time for any legal reason. At some organizations, part-time employees may exist somewhere in between. They may receive some benefits and protections even though they are expected to put in less than a full work week.

A casual worker is paid by the hour and just for the hours worked in a pay period. Unless there is an agreement that specifically grants additional benefits, a casual worker can be terminated at any time for any lawful reason.

Consultants, workers provided by a temporary employment agency, and certain other types of members of the workforce are usually under your organization's control. They must follow rules and procedures even though they are paid by and receive benefits from a third party.

Don't make assumptions about worker status. Get the facts from personnel and legal experts. A cautious approach might save you a great deal of trouble and expense in defending against claims made by an unhappy worker.

As with all of the employment problems we're dealing with in this book, it is essential that new hires be given precise and specific descriptions of their working hours as part of the employee manual or as an element of their job descriptions.

Make sure all terms are defined:

Sick days: These are days when the employee is too ill or otherwise not physically able to come to work. In very few companies would it make sense to demand that someone who has the flu must come to work; to begin with, this person is not likely to be very productive. The worker might also become a walking infection zone, spreading disease to coworkers and customers. Similarly, it may be counterproductive to insist that an employee who is taking a medicine causing sleepiness or tremors come to work, particularly if that worker operates a dangerous machine (including a car or truck).

Some companies offer a fixed number of sick days per year. Unused days may expire at the end of each year, or they may roll over to the next. Other companies may be more flexible, allowing a nearly unlimited number of sick days providing the employee is able to document a health reason for not coming to work.

But one important distinction here is that sick days are not intended as extra holidays. An employee is not supposed to use a sick day to arrange a three-day weekend or to add a day or two on to the beginning or end of a vacation. That should be clearly explained to employees, and a supervisor should be on the lookout for staffers who seem to regularly come down with the sniffles around holidays or vacations.

Personal days: Almost all of us have multiple roles in life. We are employees, but we are also husbands or wives, mothers or fathers, sons or daughters. We may also be involved in community organizations that are supported or endorsed by the employer.

One way in which companies and organizations have tried to be sensitive to the needs of their employees while still maintaining the integrity (and necessity) of sick days is to grant a specified number of personal days, which can be used for any need. Again, these days may be ones that accrue over time, or they may go away at the end of each year.

The employer also has the right to insist that personal days not be taken at particular times of the year, not be taken in large bunches, or not be taken as an extension of a vacation period. All these limitations are possible, providing the specifics of the policy are clearly laid out in the employee manual or other documents given to members of staff.

Vacation days: Nearly every organization grants employees the right to take a specified number of days to travel to a beach, the mountains, or family gatherings, or to stay around home and do nothing at all.

No explanation of place, companion, or personal activities is necessary, but the employer does have the right to define a policy that prohibits vacation time during periods when all hands are needed on deck. Likewise, the employer can require that supervisors make certain that requests for time off do not interfere with important short-term or long-term goals of the company.

In other words, not everyone will be able to ask for two weeks in mid-July to go to the beach or to choose the best week for snow skiing.

At many businesses and organizations, the vacation time off per year grows with length of service. Some organizations may permit vacation time to be banked away if not used—to allow for longer vacations in future years or to accrue extra weeks of paid time when an employee retires or leaves for another job.

Other organizations may not want to have that sort of a liability on their books; among the reasons for this is the complexity of accounting for unused vacation time. As a manager, are you comfortable with the possibility of having to find funds in your budget next year to pay for two weeks of vacation time not taken five years ago? (Consider the fact that pay rates generally go up over time, adding to the dent in the budget.)

Required overtime: Depending on state laws and collective bargaining agreements, an employer may be allowed to require workers to come in early, stay late, or come in on a weekend or holiday or day off. Once again, the policy has to be carefully spelled out in the employee manual, and it has to follow laws and agreements that provide for compensatory time off, overtime pay, or a combination of both.

A WORD to the WISE

If your company or institution does not have a written policy as well as evidence that the policy is explained to new hires—and to all employees any time there is a material change in the policy—then you are in a very weak position when it comes to disciplining or dismissing a problematic worker. You can't accuse someone of violating a policy when the existence of that policy and adherence to it is not clearly made an element of the job.

Here's a summary of three essential elements to a time-off policy:

1. The policy has to be carefully and clearly defined before it is put into effect.
2. The policy has to be distributed to all affected employees, with supervisors available to explain all of its elements.
3. The policy has to be applied consistently to all affected employees. Granting an exception that is not specifically covered in the policy opens a loophole more than wide enough for an unhappy employee to drive a lawsuit through.

Unexcused Absences

We will now assume that all of the employees under your supervision have been properly informed of the company or institutional policy about work hours and absenteeism. Let's consider now how a worker can get on the wrong side of an employee evaluation on the issue of absenteeism:

Abuse of sick time: If an employee regularly calls in sick on the day before a holiday or has a pattern of sudden "illness" that strikes only on Fridays or Mondays, the employer has a right to ask for an explanation or (if the written policy specifies and health privacy law permits) for documentation from a doctor or other health-care provider.

Abuse of personal time: Although the policy should allow for situations such as a parent who needs to take a day off to care for a sick child, it is also reasonable for the employer to set limits and to ask that—with the exception of true emergencies—personal days do not conflict with the organization's core mission.

Abuse of vacation time: As with personal time, the employer has the right to ask that time off be taken when it can best be handled by the organization. This might be defined by a calendar that lists allowable vacation periods, or the employee might be required to seek and receive approval for days requested.

At certain organizations, another form of abuse of vacation time is when a worker does not make use of accrued days. A company may require that vacation time be used in the year in which it is earned, that there be a limit on the days held in the "bank," or that, after a point, vacation days be traded in for their cash equivalent.

Absence from duty: If the employee manual gives advance notice of this possibility, the shipping department can be summoned to work the weekend before Christmas to get holiday orders out the door, or the accounting department may be required to put in extra hours at tax season. These are reasonable demands. Employees who work these extra hours are, of course, entitled to extra pay, compensatory time off, or both. An employee who does not cooperate can be penalized.

Meetings and Conferences
Somewhere out there is someone who loves to go to meetings, training sessions, marketing presentations, and

conferences. Then there are the rest of us, who attend because these are necessary elements of our job.

The larger and more diverse the organization (in the scope of its products and services or in breadth of its geographic distribution or presence), the more likely that meetings are common. Organizations that are subject to the increasingly demanding requirements of government regulations on financial disclosure, employment practices, and personal privacy are most likely to conduct formal training and compliance meetings that are part of an essential audit trail for business practices.

Attendance at all mandatory meetings and conferences is also an element of the contract between employer and employee. Unless a gathering is listed as optional or if an employee is specifically excused from attendance, going to a meeting is part of the job—and an element of attendance is punctuality.

As the great modern philosopher Woody Allen once observed, "Eighty percent of success is showing up." To that we might add, "The other 20 percent is to be prepared."

For supervisors, here are some of the elements of employment related to meetings and conferences:

- The organization's general policy about mandatory meetings and conferences has to be carefully and clearly defined before it is put into effect.
- When a meeting is scheduled, invitees have to be notified directly or through their supervisors with full details on date, time, place, and subject.
- If a meeting is mandatory, employees should be informed of that fact, and if there are provisions for

alternatives to attendance (teleconferences, Web participation, or makeup sessions), that should be included in the memo.

- If an employee is scheduled for business travel away from the office or has been granted vacation or personal time off, the meeting invitation should indicate a process to notify the convener of the meeting.
- The policy has to be applied consistently to all affected employees.

In many organizations, the introduction of computer-based calendars as well as internal Web pages and e-mail makes it easy for managers to issue invitations to meetings and to monitor receipt of messages and responses. Those same electronic calendars can be used by managers to determine—before a meeting date and time is set—whether all affected employees are available to attend.

Once a meeting has been scheduled, the employer has to right to expect the following consequences:

- Invited employees show up, and are on time
- Any requested materials or reports be submitted or brought to the meeting as requested
- Staffers are prepared to answer questions or otherwise participate in the meeting, as outlined in the invitation or on the basis of their ordinary work assignments and responsibilities

The Late Mr. Jones

Bill Jones is a mid-level advertising copywriter for a retail company. His job description calls on him to work ordinary office hours, Monday through Friday from 9 A.M. until 5 P.M., with a thirty-minute break for lunch.

That's the schedule, and it is consistently applied to all staffers with similar jobs at the same location. (The company's West Coast office requires that some of its employees show up at 6 A.M. so that they can be at their phones and computer screens for roughly the same hours as their fellow workers in New York; they're allowed to go home at 2 P.M. Others in the West Coast department are asked to work from 10 A.M. to 6 P.M. local time, which allows the company to have staffers on duty twelve hours per day.)

That's the deal as it was presented to Mr. Jones, and that's the way it appears on his job description. As a salaried employee, he does not have to punch a time clock or fill out a weekly time sheet.

In any busy office, the start of the day is often a bit informal. There's no bell that rings at 9 A.M., and there's no sudden onrush of customers coming through the front door. More common is a situation in which employees arrive a few minutes early or a few minutes after the official start. They pick up a cup of coffee or stop by a colleague's desk for a brief greeting. Most employers are quite content to see a collegial atmosphere. But ten minutes into the day, it's normal to hear the clicking of keyboards and business telephone calls going on in all corners of the workplace.

Bill, however, is conspicuous by his absence. Almost every day, his computer screen is dark, and his phone is unanswered until twenty, thirty, or even forty-five minutes after everyone else is busy.

It's been a long time since anyone has raised an eyebrow about his tardiness. When they did, he would offer one or another excuse: The traffic to the train station was awful, the train was late, he had to drop a personal package at the post office. His coworkers and his supervisor stopped asking.

Arriving late, though, never seems to interfere with Mr. Jones' departure schedule. In fact, it can be dangerous to stand between his desk and the doorway. Five or ten minutes before 5 P.M., as most of the other employees are beginning to tidy up their desks and preparing to leave, Mr. Jones is moving with great speed toward the exit. There's little need for others to check their watches: The moving blur means it is 4:50 P.M.

Verbal Notification

Bill, I'd like to speak with you about your working hours. According to the employee manual, the regular working hours for your position are Monday through Friday from 9 A.M. to 5 P.M. with a thirty-minute lunch break.

You are a salaried employee, and we don't have a time clock. However, it is apparent to me and to other managers that you are often late to arrive, and it also seems that you are one of the first to leave at the end of the day.

We consider you a valued employee and we greatly appreciate the quality of your work. But in an organization, sometimes appearances are as important as performance.

Is there any reason why you cannot regularly be at work during ordinary business hours?

Optional: Is there anything we can do as an organization to assist you in meeting the requirements of your job? We do offer flex-time arrangements to some of our employees if you'd like to discuss a slightly different schedule, such as 9:30 A.M. to 5:30 P.M., or 8:30 A.M. to 4:30 P.M.

MEMO TO FILE: Noting a request for action

Confidential: Personnel matter
Date: January 15, 20xx
Manager:
Regarding employee: Bill Jones
Subject: Working hours

I met this morning with Bill Jones to discuss his working hours. I told him that it was apparent to me and to other managers, including Jay Witzel in Marketing, that he often arrives fifteen to thirty minutes late in the morning and seems to be one of the first to leave at the end of the day.

I told Mr. Jones that we are happy with the quality of his work and we very much want to see him succeed here and advance within the organization. However, I advised him that in an organization, sometimes appearances are as important as performance.

I reviewed with him the section of his job description that deals with working hours and the general policy that is laid out in the employee manual. We discussed the fact that the conversation we were having was not a reprimand.

I asked him if there was any reason why he could not regularly be at work during ordinary business hours.

Mr. Jones told me that because of where he lives, he has found it difficult to find a reliable commuting schedule that would allow him to be in the office at 9 A.M. He said the train schedule at the end of the day is also not well suited to his commute.

I advised him that, with the permission of his supervisor and manager, we would be willing to adjust his working hours to a flex-time schedule. I suggested he research his commuting options and propose working hours such as 8:30 A.M. to 4:30 P.M., or 9:30 A.M. to 5:30 P.M.

I asked him to make a proposal by the end of this week, January 18.

MEMO TO FILE: Offer of assistance

Confidential: Personnel matter
Date: January 18, 20xx
Manager:
Regarding employee: Bill Jones
Subject: Adjustment to job description working hours

Bill Jones has requested that his ordinary working hours be adjusted to take into account train schedules, which make it difficult for him to be at his desk by 9 A.M.

I have discussed his situation with his supervisor, Jay Witzel, and we have no problem with changing Bill's schedule to flex time. Effective immediately, his working hours are from 9:30 A.M. to 5:30 P.M.

We did discuss with Bill the fact that he must be able to adjust his schedule to attend any mandatory meetings scheduled before 9:30 A.M. We agreed to meet again in ninety days to review progress on this matter.

Please include this memo in his file. We have given Bill a copy for his own records.

PERFORMANCE EVALUATION: Acknowledging progress

Confidential: Personnel matter
Date: March 1, 20xx
Manager:
Regarding employee: Bill Jones
Subject: Adjustment to job description working hours

Mr. Jones has successfully adapted his working hours to flex time, arriving as requested by 9:30 A.M. and remaining until 5:30 P.M. This resulted from his request for an adjustment because of circumstances pertaining to his commute.

As agreed when his working hours were adjusted, he has on several occasions arrived earlier than 9:30 A.M. to attend departmental meetings or for special projects.

PERFORMANCE EVALUATION: Fails to meet expectations

Confidential: Personnel matter
Date: March 1, 20xx
Manager:
Regarding employee: Bill Jones
Subject: Adjustment to job description working hours

On January 15 of this year, Mr. Jones was advised that his supervisors felt he was not fulfilling his assigned work hours. According to his job description, he is supposed to be at his desk Monday to Friday from 9 A.M. to 5 P.M. His supervisors reported he was late in arriving most days, sometimes by as much as thirty minutes, and that he often left before 5 P.M.

Mr. Jones acknowledged to me that he was having difficulty keeping to the assigned schedule. He explained that the commuter train service from his home arrived and departed on the hour. In order to be at his desk at 9 A.M., he would have to take the train that arrived downtown at 8 A.M., and in order to stay until 5 P.M. at the end of the day, he would have to take the train that left a full hour later, at 6 P.M.

He was offered the option of flex time, which would allow him to adjust his working hours to more closely match the train schedule. He was asked to propose an adjustment by January 18. On that day we agreed to move his start time to 9:30 A.M. and set his ordinary end of day to 5:30 P.M. A copy of a memo outlining this adjustment to his job description is in Mr. Jones's personnel file.

According to his supervisors, Mr. Jones followed the new schedule for several weeks, but beginning approximately February 15, he is once again arriving and departing at times other than those in his schedule. According to notes from his department head, last week (the week of February 20 to 25) he arrived at 9:40, 9:45, 9:35, 9:50, and 9:45; in that same week, he departed each day at 4:45 P.M.)

With this performance appraisal, Mr. Jones is instructed that unless he has specific permission from his supervisor for an adjustment, he must meet his assigned schedule that requires his presence from 9:30 A.M. to 5:30 P.M. daily. He will be evaluated again on March 15.

Every employee is expected to follow the working hours of his or her job description as well as all of the elements of the code of conduct. Failure to meet these expectations can be grounds for dismissal.

WRITTEN WARNING

Confidential: Personnel matter
Date: March 1, 20xx
Manager:
Regarding employee: Bill Jones
Subject: Adjustment to job description working hours

I am writing to confirm some specific elements of the performance evaluation conducted on this date.

You have been advised that your supervisors report that you are failing to consistently meet expectations for your daily working hours. Your original job description called for a work day of 9 A.M. to 5 P.M.; on January 18, 20xx, that schedule was amended, at your request, to 9:30 A.M. to 5:30 P.M. This accommodation was made because you said this would better match the commuter train schedule from your home to work and back.

As we discussed in your performance evaluation, your supervisors report that you followed the new schedule for several weeks after it was implemented, but in the past month your arrival times have been consistently late, and you been departing early.

You were advised today that your attendance record will be closely monitored. If it is determined that you are unable to consistently meet expectations by March 15, we will refer your file to the human resources department for termination from employment. If there are further repeated problems with attendance after March 15, 20xx, we will seek immediate termination at that time.

The Lady Who Lunches

Pamela Smith is an office stalwart. She shows up at her workstation exactly on time, stays at her desk until the last minute of her assigned schedule, and rarely misses a day. But she does love to do lunch.

Her workday begins at 8:30 A.M. and ends at 5 P.M. The employee manual specifies that professionals in her position are entitled to a one-hour lunch break that can be taken any time between 11:30 A.M. and 1:30 P.M. The manual also directs employees to arrange with their managers to stagger the times they take lunch so that there is always someone available in each department.

So much for theory. In daily practice, Ms. Smith sidles toward the door every day at 11:45 A.M. and rarely makes it back before 1:15 P.M. While many of the other employees head for the nearby park to eat a sandwich brought from home or occasionally walk up the street to sit at a lunch counter, Ms. Smith seems to have a long list of friends who work in nearby stores and offices, and they dine at linen-clothed tables—except during shopping season, that is, which seems to run from Labor Day to New Year's. On regular occasions during that period, Ms. Smith struggles back to her desk carrying multiple colorful shopping bags. She's happy, tired, and late. And everyone knows.

Verbal Notification

Ms. Smith, I've asked you to meet with me to talk about your lunch breaks. According to the employee manual, you are entitled to a one-hour lunch break each day. Your supervisor has brought it to my attention that this is not the schedule you adhere to on a regular basis.

According to what I have been told, you are often away from your desk for an hour and a half, and sometimes even longer.

I'm sure you can understand that this is something that can cause disruption in the workplace and resentment from coworkers. We would prefer that you follow the work schedule.

Is there a particular reason that you have been taking this extra time off? As you know, we try to be as flexible as possible to meet the needs of our valued employees; we could discuss the possibility of extending your work day so that you come in early or work later.

MEMO TO FILE: Noting a request for action

Confidential: Personnel matter
Date: January 15, 20xx
Manager:
Regarding employee: Pamela Smith
Subject: Lunch break

I met with Ms. Smith today to discuss with her a memo I had received from her supervisor indicating that she regularly took lunch breaks that were considerably longer than the one hour specified in the employee handbook. According to the report I received, Ms. Smith was often out of the office for as long as an hour and a half or more. Because of this, her department had to change the schedules of other workers to make sure that the phones were covered at all times.

Ms. Smith said that she felt that the time detailed in the memo might be somewhat exaggerated. She said she felt that most of the time she was out of the building for lunch for no more than ten or fifteen minutes beyond her scheduled period. She assured me that she would be more attentive to the work schedule in the future. I thanked her for her promise.

Ms. Smith also said that because of a medical condition, she was limited in her ability to move, and it was for that reason that she was occasionally late in getting back to her desk after lunch breaks. She said the condition did not affect her ability to accomplish her job assignments.

MEMO TO FILE: Offer of assistance

Confidential: Personnel matter
Date: January 15, 20xx
Manager:
Regarding employee: Pamela Smith
Subject: Lunch break

I met with Ms. Smith today to discuss with her a memo I had received from her supervisor indicating that she regularly took lunch breaks that were considerably longer than the one hour allotted by the employee handbook. According to the report I received, Ms. Smith often was out of the office for as long as an hour and a half or more. Because of this, her department has had to change the schedules of other workers to make sure the phones were covered at all times.

Ms. Smith assured me that she would be more attentive to the work schedule in the future. I thanked her for her promise.

I also informed Ms. Smith that in exceptional circumstances she could seek permission from her supervisor for an extended lunch hour, with the understanding that she would make up the lost time during the same work week.

Ms. Smith said that because of a medical condition she was limited in her ability to move, and it was for that reason that she was occasionally late in getting back to her desk after lunch breaks. She said the condition did not affect her ability to accomplish her job assignments.

In keeping with the organization's employee manual, I told Ms. Smith we would do whatever we could to assist her in the performance of her job. I asked her to meet with an officer of the human resources department to discuss options, which could include extending the work day with an earlier start or a later finish to allow for a longer lunch hour.

PERFORMANCE EVALUATION: Acknowledging progress

Confidential: Personnel matter
Date: March 1, 20xx
Manager:
Regarding employee: Pamela Smith
Subject: Lunch break

In recent weeks, Ms. Smith has demonstrated commitment to following company rules in regard to the length of her lunch hour and working day. We will continue to monitor her schedule from time to time, as appropriate.

PERFORMANCE EVALUATION: Fails to meet expectations

Confidential: Personnel matter
Date: March 1, 20xx
Manager:
Regarding employee: Pamela Smith
Subject: Lunch break

Approximately six weeks ago, on January 15, I met with Ms. Smith to discuss reports from her supervisors that she was regularly taking lunch breaks that extended well beyond the one-hour period detailed in her job description. I told her that her action was causing disruption in her department because of the need to reassign other staffers to handle calls in her absence.

Ms. Smith responded that she felt the reports of her schedule were exaggerated, but she promised to curtail her lunch break to just one hour per day.

According to her supervisor, there has been little change in her break schedule since January. She continues to be away from her desk for more than an hour every day. Yesterday, February 29, she was observed leaving the office at 11:45 A.M. and returning at 1:30 P.M.

At our first meeting on this matter, I asked Ms. Smith if she wanted to request a special accommodation, such as an adjustment in her working hours. She told me that was not necessary.

Since the problem has continued, and in keeping with policies laid out in the employee manual, I have advised the human resources department that I am placing Ms. Smith under formal notice that effective today, her lunch break will be monitored and recorded daily. She is expected to follow the official work schedule that is part of her job description unless she has specific permission for an exception.

We will review her working schedule again in two weeks, on March 15, and at regular intervals after that. A continued disregard for the official work schedule will be considered grounds for dismissal.

WRITTEN WARNING

Confidential: Personnel matter
Date: March 1, 20xx
Manager:
Regarding employee: Pamela Smith
Subject: Lunch break

I am writing to confirm some specific elements of the performance evaluation conducted on this date.

As I informed you today, we are not satisfied with the fact that you continue to take lunch breaks significantly longer than the sixty minutes allowed in your job description. In previous discussions, we have offered an adjustment to your work schedule. You have instead informed us that you would follow the rules as they apply to your job.

You were advised today that your attendance record will be closely monitored. If it is determined that you are consistently unable to meet expectations by March 15, we will refer your file to the human resources department for termination from employment. If there are further repeated problems with attendance after March 15, 20xx, we will seek immediate termination at that time.

The Lost Weekend

We're just guessing here, but it seems as if Waylon Brown has a most interesting medical condition. Let's call it lostweekenditis.

Here are the symptoms. Nearly every time a scheduled holiday approaches, Mr. Brown picks up the sniffles, a stomachache, a migraine, or some combination of the three. It's nothing serious, just enough to keep him away from the office the day before the scheduled three-day Labor Day weekend or to prevent him from returning on Boxing Day after Christmas.

Many of his coworkers don't even realize he has this medical problem; they may not recall that it reoccurs with such regularity. But one thing is certain: They do notice each time he calls in sick when everyone else has made it to work on either side of a holiday. It's the sort of thing that eats away at the morale of those who have a healthy regard for the responsibilities of their job.

Verbal Notification

It has been brought to my attention that on at least three occasions during the past year, you have taken a sick day at the start or end of a holiday period. I confirmed this with the human resources department. We noted this pattern coinciding with the Thanksgiving, Christmas, and President's Day breaks.

It appears that this is a pattern, in violation of the rules detailed in the employee manual, which require that personal days not be scheduled to extend a holiday period without permission in advance.

It is also company policy that sick days only be used for actual instances of medical problems or appointments. Unused sick days can be converted to personal days at the end of each calendar year. The employee manual requires that your supervisor approve personal days in advance so that they do not cause an undue burden on others. Finally, supervisors must approve all vacation requests.

We consider you a valued employee and hope to have your contributions for many years to come. I hope you can understand, though, that the rules concerning attendance are intended to allow all employees a reasonable number of days off; departmental managers are required to maintain minimum levels of staffing throughout the year.

Confidential: Personnel matter
Date: January 18, 20xx
Manager:
Regarding employee: Waylon Brown
Subject: Holiday work pattern

I met with Mr. Brown today and discussed with him what appears to be a pattern of abuse of the organization's policy regarding scheduling of extra days off around holiday periods.

I discussed with Mr. Brown attendance records provided by the human resources department that showed at least three occasions during the past twelve months on which he had taken a sick day at the start or end of a holiday period. The days were taken at the Thanksgiving, Christmas, and President's Day breaks.

I reviewed with Mr. Brown the organization's employee manual, which states that personal days are not to be scheduled to extend a holiday period without advance permission from a supervisor or department head. Similarly, supervisors must approve all vacation requests.

I also made clear that it is our policy that sick days may only be used for actual instances of medical problems or appointments.

Finally, I reminded Mr. Brown that the employee manual allows unused sick days to be converted to personal days at the end of each calendar year. The employee manual requires that a supervisor approve personal days in advance so that they do not cause an undue burden on others.

Mr. Brown said that he felt that the sick days he had taken were all legitimate but promised to follow all of the guidelines in the employee manual regarding days off.

MEMO TO FILE: Offer of assistance

Confidential: Personnel matter
Date: January 18, 20xx
Manager:
Regarding employee: Waylon Brown
Subject: Holiday work pattern

I met with Mr. Brown today and discussed with him what appears to be a pattern of abuse of the organization's policy regarding scheduling of extra days off around holiday periods. We discussed the rules as spelled out in the employee handbook.

I told Mr. Brown that it was a violation of company policy to take a sick day for reasons other than medical necessity; unused sick days can be converted to personal days at the end of each calendar year. A supervisor or department head must approve personal days off in advance.

I offered to set up a session with the human resources department to review the employee handbook and answer any questions; Mr. Brown said this was not necessary. He said he would follow the rules regarding days off from work.

PERFORMANCE EVALUATION: Acknowledging progress

Confidential: Personnel matter
Date: March 1, 20xx
Manager:
Regarding employee: Waylon Brown
Subject: Holiday work pattern

According to supervisors, Mr. Brown has demonstrated full cooperation with organizational rules regarding vacation and personal days since January. We will continue to monitor his schedule for the next twelve months.

PERFORMANCE EVALUATION: Fails to meet expectations

Confidential: Personnel matter
Date: March 1, 20xx
Manager:
Regarding employee: Waylon Brown
Subject: Holiday work pattern

According to supervisors, we continue to see a pattern that indicates Mr. Brown's failure to meet our expectations regarding use of personal and sick days.

On January 18 of this year, we met to review the organization's policies regarding days off and a recurring pattern of what appeared to be misuse of sick days for personal purposes. In the period since then, according to supervisors, Mr. Brown has called in sick on the Friday before the start of the President's Day weekend and on the Wednesday at its end.

It is our policy that sick days may only be used for actual instances of medical problems or appointments and not to extend vacation or holiday periods. The employee manual allows the company to request certification of illness or proof of a medical appointment. The nature of an illness or injury is considered private information unless it has a direct impact on an employee's ability to perform his or her duties or it poses a threat to others in the workplace. All this was reviewed with Mr. Brown in meetings in January of this year.

At the meeting tomorrow, we will review the policy on sick days, personal days, and vacation days. It will not be our intention to revisit each of the previous instances on which Mr. Brown has been absent from work on days surrounding holidays. However, from this point forward, it will be our intention to closely monitor Mr. Brown's use of sick days, personal days, and vacation days.

Mr. Brown has been advised that we expect him to follow all of the rules regarding days off as well as all other elements of the employee manual and code of conduct. Further problems related to observance of attendance rules may be used as the basis for dismissal.

I have scheduled a meeting with Mr. Brown and his supervisor for tomorrow, March 2, at 2 P.M. to discuss what appears to be a continuing pattern of violation of use of sick days.

Confidential: Personnel matter
Date: March 1, 20xx
Manager:
Regarding employee: Waylon Brown
Subject: Holiday work pattern

I am writing to inform you that I have scheduled a meeting with you and your supervisor for tomorrow, March 2, at 2 P.M. to discuss what appears to be a continuing pattern of violation of use of sick days.

On January 18 of this year we met to review the organization's policies regarding days off and a recurring pattern of what appeared to be misuse of sick days for personal purposes. In the period since then, you have called in sick on the Friday before the start of the Presidents' Day weekend and on the Wednesday at its end.

As we discussed in January, it is our policy that sick days may only be used for actual instances of medical problems or appointments and not to extend vacation or holiday periods. The employee manual allows the company to request certification of illness or proof of a medical appointment. The nature of an illness or injury is considered private information unless it has a direct impact on your ability to perform your duties or it poses a threat to others in the workplace.

At the meeting tomorrow, we will review the policy on sick days, personal days, and vacation days. It will not be our intention to revisit each of the previous instances on which you have been absent from work on days surrounding holidays. However, from this point forward, we will closely monitor your use of sick days, personal days, and vacation days.

We value your work for the company and hope you will have many years of productive service with us. We are advising you that we expect you to follow all of the rules regarding days off as well as all other elements of the employee manual and code of conduct. Further problems related to observance of attendance rules may be used as the basis for dismissal.

Absent Without Leave

Knickerbocker Knick-Knack Company's busiest time arrives in early November of each year. The factory has fulfilled all of the orders for Christmas doodads, and now it is time to push the product out the door to customers.

Everyone in the shipping department knows he or she is expected to put in overtime for a few weeks. Even the clerical staff is regularly called upon to help load boxes, print shipping labels, and keep the accounting system current.

Many of the employees enjoy the crunch. Company policy (and state and federal law) offers hourly workers overtime pay or compensatory time off when things are less hectic. For those workers, the extra hours are a way to earn extra cash or build up extended vacation periods. It's also part of the corporate culture. Some of the management come in to work, and the company president usually pitches in for a few hours and orders a truck full of pizzas.

But one employee, Arlene Green, draws the line at overtime. Oh, she may come in an hour early and stay an hour late for a few days here and there. But she makes it clear, without offering any specific detail, that her family and other personal responsibilities are more important to her than working through the weekend or staying late at night, free pizza or not.

Verbal Notification

Mrs. Green, I need to speak with you about your lack of availability for overtime work during the holiday season.

The employee manual states that a supervisor can require staffers to work extra hours or extra days. The specific language says we must give "reasonable notice" in advance. As a practice, our managers have been asked to give at least three days' advance notice whenever possible.

Your job description includes a section that notes the period of time from Thanksgiving through Christmas and into the first week of January as our busiest retail period. We do not grant vacation or personal days off during that period, and your job description specifically states that you can expect to be required to put in extra hours. As you know, staffers are eligible to choose overtime pay or compensatory time off or both.

Your supervisor has informed me that you have refused all overtime requirements in recent weeks.

Is there some particular problem that I need to be made aware of that makes it impossible for you meet the needs of your job description during the holiday period?

Would you like to discuss an adjustment in your regular working hours that would allow you to meet your supervisor's expectations for extra hours during the holiday period?

Confidential: Personnel matter
Date: December 1, 20xx
Manager:
Regarding employee: Arlene Green
Subject: Overtime availability

I met with Mrs. Green today to discuss her recent lack of availability for overtime assignments during the holiday period. I reviewed with her the fact that the employee manual states that a supervisor can require staffers to work extra hours or extra days. I referred to specific language in the manual that says we must give "reasonable notice" in advance and told her that our company's ordinary interpretation of that section of the manual is that we give at least three days' advance notice whenever possible.

The job description for the position held by Mrs. Green includes a section that notes the period of time from Thanksgiving through Christmas and into the first week of January as our busiest retail period, and it says employees can expect to be required to put in overtime hours during that time of year. It goes on to state that without special permission, the organization does not grant vacation or personal days off during that period.

I discussed with Mrs. Green reports I received from her supervisor that she has refused all overtime requirements in recent weeks.

She responded that her family obligations, including difficulty in obtaining care for her young child, make it difficult for her to work beyond her ordinary hours.

I told Mrs. Green that we understood her situation and valued her as an employee but asked that she investigate ways in which she could meet the obligations that are identified in the job description. I asked her to meet with me again on December 3 to seek a satisfactory solution.

MEMO TO FILE: Offer of assistance

Confidential: Personnel matter
Date: December 1, 20xx
Manager:
Regarding employee: Arlene Green
Subject: Overtime availability

I have asked the human resources department to schedule a meeting tomorrow with Arlene Green and her supervisor to explore options that would allow her to satisfy the company's need for extra working hours by all marketing and sales staff during the holiday period.

The job description for the position held by Mrs. Green includes a section that notes the period of time from Thanksgiving through Christmas and into the first week of January as our busiest retail period and says that employees can expect to be required to put in overtime hours during that time of year. It goes on to state that without special permission, the organization does not grant vacation or personal days off during that period.

I reviewed with Mrs. Green provisions in the employee manual that state that a supervisor can require staffers to work extra hours or extra days. I referred to specific language in the manual that says we must give "reasonable notice" in advance and told her that our company's ordinary interpretation of that section of the manual is that we give at least three days' advance notice whenever possible.

She responded that her family obligations, including difficulty in obtaining care for her young child, make it difficult for her to work beyond her ordinary hours.

I told Mrs. Green that we understood her situation and valued her as an employee but asked that she investigate ways in which she could meet the obligations that are identified in the job description. I have asked the human resources department to schedule a meeting to discuss Mrs. Green's work schedule and to discuss ways in which the company can assist her in finding child care and other solutions. The human resources staff is aware of other employees with similar situations and can advise solutions.

I reiterated that it is important that we have full coverage by employees during the holiday period but will make every effort to see that every employee is given the opportunity to manage requirements of the workplace with the least disruption to family obligations.

I asked Mrs. Green to meet with me again on December 3 to discuss her work schedule for the remainder of the holiday season.

PERFORMANCE EVALUATION: Acknowledging progress

Confidential: Personnel matter
Date: January 15, 20xx
Manager:
Regarding employee: Arlene Green
Subject: Overtime availability

Mrs. Green demonstrated her commitment to the company this past December when she worked with her supervisor and the human resources department to change her working hours for the holiday period. She was asked to meet with her departmental head after she declined holiday overtime because of difficulty in obtaining care for her young child after regular working hours.

In cooperation with her supervisor and the head of her department, Mrs. Green worked out a schedule that was put in place for the eight-week holiday period. This schedule permitted her to take a two-hour break in the late afternoon to bring her child from his day-care center to a relative's home then return to the office for a night shift three days per week. Her workload was adjusted to permit the new schedule.

I have scheduled a meeting for September 15 of next year to allow for advance planning for the next holiday period. I have asked Mrs. Green and her supervisor to meet before that date to come up with an acceptable plan.

PERFORMANCE EVALUATION: Fails to meet expectations

Confidential: Personnel matter
Date: January 15, 20xx
Manager:
Regarding employee: Arlene Green
Subject: Overtime availability

On December 1, I met with Mrs. Green to discuss her recent lack of availability for overtime assignments during the holiday period. I reviewed with her the fact that the employee manual states that a supervisor can require staffers to work extra hours or extra days. I referred to specific language in the manual that says we must give "reasonable notice" in advance and told her that our company's ordinary interpretation of that section of the manual is that we give at least three days' advance notice whenever possible.

The job description for the position held by Mrs. Green includes a section that notes the period of time from Thanksgiving through Christmas and into the first week of January as our busiest retail period and says employees can expect to be required to put in overtime hours during that time of year. It goes on to state that without special permission, the organization does not grant vacation or personal days off during that period.

I discussed with Mrs. Green reports I received from her supervisor that she has refused all overtime requirements in recent weeks.

She responded that her family obligations, including difficulty in obtaining care for her young child, make it difficult for her to work beyond her ordinary hours.

Despite requests by Mrs. Green's supervisor and offers that I made to involve the human resources department in seeking adjustments to her schedule or assisting her in obtaining childcare, Mrs. Green has continued to decline all overtime work. She did not show up for scheduled overtime periods and did not accept any optional time slots that were posted for her department.

I am advising Mrs. Green that a refusal to be available for a reasonable number of overtime hours in the holiday season may result in termination of her employment.

I will schedule a meeting with Mrs. Green for September of this year to discuss her preparations for the holiday season.

WRITTEN WARNING

Confidential: Personnel matter
Date: January 15, 20xx
Manager:
Regarding employee: Arlene Green
Subject: Overtime availability

I am writing to advise you that your lack of availability for overtime during the recently concluded holiday period was not in keeping with the terms of your job description and the company code of conduct.

Despite requests by your supervisor and offers I made to involve human resources in adjusting your schedule or assisting you in obtaining child care, you declined all overtime work. You did not show up for scheduled overtime periods and did not accept any optional time slots posted for your department.

We consider you to be a valuable and capable employee and hope that, with sufficient advance notice of overtime periods, this will not occur again this year or in coming years. With this memo, I am advising you that a refusal to be available for a reasonable number of overtime hours in the holiday season may result in termination of your employment.

I will schedule a meeting with you for September of this year to discuss your preparations for the holiday season.

We've Got to Start Meeting Like This

The sales force meets every Wednesday morning at 9 A.M. Everyone in the marketing, advertising, and sales departments is expected to attend. It's on the schedule, reminders are sent out by e-mail every Monday, and there are free doughnuts.

The department head uses the meeting for a number of purposes: to introduce new products or services, to listen to individual or group reports, and to fire up the troops with contests and promotions. It is also a time for the various interrelated departments to share information about their activities, plans, and accomplishments.

For many employees, this is an opportunity to make suggestions or make themselves known to executives who regularly attend. They prepare themselves for the meeting the day before, bringing notes and reports. Members of the staff also know they may be called upon without advance notice to answer a question about their area of expertise or about their personal or departmental contributions to the organization's overall performance.

It would probably be difficult to find any staffer who could honestly say he or she enjoys meetings or who wouldn't jump at an opportunity to be somewhere else doing something else on Wednesday mornings. But like a visit to the dentist, it's something that has to happen.

Manny Kant doesn't buy into the deal. He hates meetings, avoids any preparation, and does his best to blend in with the potted plants when he's in the room. When his supervisor began to assess his performance, he went back over the office schedule and noticed that Mr. Kant had somehow managed to be out on sales calls, at off-site conferences, and otherwise AWOL for an unusually large percentage of Wednesdays over the course of the past two years.

Verbal Notification

I've asked you to meet with me to discuss a recurring problem that has been developing over the past year. Your supervisor and departmental head have informed me that your attendance at the Wednesday group meeting has been sporadic and undependable. As you know, attendance at that meeting is mandatory. All staffers are asked not to schedule any activities outside of the office during that time without permission. We also discourage employees from taking personal days off on Wednesday.

When you do show up for these meetings, I am informed you are often ill prepared and sometimes uncooperative or dismissive of the purposes of the session. Your absence and reluctance to participate has been noticed not just by your supervisors but by your peers as well.

We consider these meetings to be an important element of planning and communication within the organization, an opportunity to share information and strategize about upcoming initiatives.

I want you to understand that we expect you to attend and participate in all of the mandatory departmental and organization-wide meetings. Please keep in touch with your supervisor if you anticipate any situations that would cause you to be absent.

MEMO TO FILE: Noting a request for action

Confidential: Personnel matter
Date: January 18, 20xx
Manager:
Regarding employee: Manny Kant
Subject: Attendance at departmental meetings

I met with Mr. Kant today to discuss his attendance record at departmental meetings.

According to his department head, Mr. Kant has missed at least half the meetings held in the past six months. When he has shown up for meetings, he has neither contributed to the discussion nor offered any information on initiatives in his own group. His attitude is reported to be openly uncooperative or dismissive of the purposes of the session.

I reminded Mr. Kant that attendance at weekly Wednesday morning meetings is mandatory and that all staffers are asked not to schedule any activities outside of the office during that time without permission. I told Mr. Kant that we expected him to participate in the meetings and to be prepared to answer questions about his activities and initiatives in his department. We consider these meetings to be an important element of planning and communication within the organization, an opportunity to share information and strategize about upcoming initiatives.

I reviewed with Mr. Kant other elements of his job description and the employee manual, including sections that discourage employees from taking personal days that would conflict with mandatory meetings. I also reminded him that any staffer who misses a meeting for any reason is asked to meet with his or her supervisor to review any missed announcements or requests.

I have asked the departmental supervisor to monitor Mr. Kant's attendance at upcoming meetings and to report to me any further absences or problems.

PERFORMANCE EVALUATION: Acknowledging progress

Confidential: Personnel matter
Date: February 15, 20xx
Manager:
Regarding employee: Manny Kant
Subject: Attendance at departmental meetings

After a meeting with his supervisor in January of this year regarding his absence from a number of departmental meetings, Mr. Kant has attended all subsequent meetings and made a noticeable effort to make meaningful contributions to discussions. We appreciate his attention to this element of his job description as well as his other efforts on behalf of the organization.

Confidential: Personnel matter
Date: February 15, 20xx
Manager:
Regarding employee: Manny Kant
Subject: Attendance at departmental meetings

After a meeting with his supervisor in January of this year regarding his absence from a number of departmental meetings, Mr. Kant was reminded that attendance at these sessions is mandatory. Further, he was asked to better prepare himself to answer questions and to make presentations when requested by his manager.

We consider departmental meetings to be an important element of planning and communication within the organization, an opportunity to share information and strategize about upcoming initiatives.

I reviewed with Mr. Kant other elements of his job description and the employee manual, including sections that discourage employees from taking personal days off that would conflict with mandatory meetings. I also reminded him that any staffer who misses a meeting because of illness, a scheduled vacation, or an approved absence for other reasons is asked to meet with his or her supervisor to review any announcements or requests missed.

I was informed today that Mr. Kant has missed three of the four departmental meetings since January 18.

With this performance evaluation, Mr. Kant is hereby notified that any further absence from a departmental meeting without being excused in advance by a supervisor will be considered as grounds for immediate termination from employment.

WRITTEN WARNING

Confidential: Personnel matter
Date: February 15, 20xx
Manager:
Regarding employee: Manny Kant
Subject: Attendance at departmental meetings

According to your supervisor and department head, you have shown an ongoing disregard for the element of your job description that requires regular attendance at weekly departmental meetings. As you know, I spoke with you about this matter in January of this year and informed you that your supervisor would monitor your attendance at meetings and report back to me regarding this manner.

According to your departmental supervisor, you have missed three of the four meetings since this matter was first reported on January 18.

I am writing to inform you that we consider your lack of attention to this element of your job description to be a very serious breach of responsibility. With this memo, you are hereby notified that any further absence from a departmental meeting without being excused in advance by a supervisor will be considered as grounds for immediate termination from employment.

Chapter 2

DEADLINES OR GOALS

ALMOST EVERYTHING WE do at work involves some form of deadline or goal. A report has to be delivered before a scheduled meeting or assessment. Manufacturing or sales departments set goals for units built or sold to customers. Support personnel are expected to accomplish a certain number of tasks or maintain a particular level of quality over time.

Sometimes the deadline or goal is associated with a particular set of job-related skills. An employee might reasonably be expected to learn how to perform a new set of tasks, attain certification in a formal program, or address some other need identified in a performance evaluation.

As with other elements of the implied contract between the employer and employee, it is not improper to expect workers to meet reasonable deadlines, to keep themselves current on new products, technologies, or skills, or to improve their performance over time. This is true as long as all staffers performing essentially the same tasks are treated in the same manner—or, put the other way around, as long as an individual employee is not treated in a discriminatory fashion.

An employer, as part of the evaluation process that is common to all staff, can require certain efforts be made to improve performance in meeting deadlines and goals.

Over Her Head

Ellie Verbatim is always behind schedule and seems to forever be overwhelmed by her portfolio of assignments. She very rarely meets deadlines or goals, and when she does, the quality of her work is much lower than that of her coworkers.

No one, though, could fault her for trying. She is at her desk early each day and often works past regular hours.

Her supervisor has met with her on numerous occasions, enlisting the assistance of coworkers in helping Ms. Verbatim attempt to organize and prioritize her tasks. Together they have made certain that her workload is equitable and that the particular portfolio does not include any clients who are more difficult to deal with than others.

But eighteen months into her current position, Ms. Verbatim continues to lag behind.

Verbal Notification

I've asked you to meet with me to discuss your difficulties in meeting deadlines and goals.

Everyone here, including all of your supervisors and managers, respects your diligence and willingness to work. We value you very highly and very much want you to succeed.

However, we continue to have problems with the timeliness and quality of your work. I know that you have met with your supervisor a number of times to discuss ways in which you could become more organized and productive.

At this point, though, I think it is important that we try a more formal approach. I'd like you to meet with a representative of the human resources department next week to discuss options for training or the possibility of a reassignment to other responsibilities.

MEMO TO FILE: Noting a request for action

Confidential: Personnel matter
Date: January 15, 20xx
Manager:
Regarding employee: Ellie Verbatim
Subject: Organizational skills

I met on this date with Ellie Verbatim to discuss continuing problems with the timeliness and quality of her work.

I told Ms. Verbatim that all her supervisors and managers respected her commitment to her job and the amount of time and effort she put into her work. However, despite several informal attempts by her supervisor to assist her in becoming more organized and productive, the results of her efforts do not meet the expectations that are laid out in her job description.

I have asked the human resources department to schedule a meeting with Ms. Verbatim within the next week to discuss possible training programs, coaching, and adaptations we might make to seek improvements in her organizational skills and productivity. I have asked human resources to keep me informed about their suggestions in this matter. I have also requested that Ms. Verbatim's supervisor brief me once a month on her progress.

We have every hope that this training will help improve Ms. Verbatim's skills. However, if her present work quality does not improve, it may be necessary to transfer her to a different job or initiate the process to terminate her employment.

MEMO TO FILE: Offer of assistance

Confidential: Personnel matter
Date: January 18, 20xx
Manager:
Regarding employee: Ellie Verbatim
Subject: Organizational skills

I was notified today of the results of a meeting between Ellie Verbatim and Diane Potter of the human resources department. This meeting was held at my request to explore training programs, coaching, and adaptation that might be available to assist Ms. Verbatim in improving her organizational skills and work product.

Mrs. Potter informed me that she has recommended we engage the services of an outside consultant who specializes in personal tutoring on job skills. Ms. Verbatim has promised her full commitment to the project. Attached to this memo is approval of a budget for payment for twenty-five hours of training to be conducted over a five-week period.

I have asked Mrs. Potter to keep me posted on the progress of training, which should begin by early February.

I have put on the schedule for April 1 a conference to include Ms. Verbatim, her departmental supervisor, Mrs. Potter, and myself to assess progress at that time.

PERFORMANCE EVALUATION: Acknowledging progress

Confidential: Personnel matter
Date: April 1, 20xx
Manager:
Regarding employee: Ellie Verbatim
Subject: Organizational skills

Ms. Verbatim has demonstrated in recent months considerable improvement in the quality of her work and her ability to deliver projects on schedule. She has worked closely with the human resources department and an outside trainer to enhance her skills.

We will continue to monitor her progress in this part of her job description.

PERFORMANCE EVALUATION: Fails to meet expectations

Confidential: Personnel matter
Date: April 1, 20xx
Manager:
Regarding employee: Ellie Verbatim
Subject: Organizational skills

In recent months I have expressed concern to Ms. Verbatim about her inability to produce work of acceptable quality and to meet deadlines. She met with her supervisor on several occasions to discuss this informally and seek guidance. On January 18, per my instructions, she met with Diane Potter of the human resources department to explore training programs, coaching, and adaptation that might be available to assist her in improving her organizational skills and work product.

Mrs. Potter recommended we engage the services of an outside consultant who specializes in personal tutoring on job skills. Ms. Verbatim promised her full commitment to the project. The consultant was engaged for twenty-five hours of personal training, conducted over a five-week period.

Unfortunately, reports by Ms. Verbatim's supervisor (attached to this memo) inform me that there has been little or no significant improvement in the quality of work. Ms. Verbatim also continues to have an inability to meet deadlines.

With this performance evaluation, as per the employee manual, I am notifying Ms. Verbatim that I will meet with her supervisor in fifteen days, on April 16, to formally review her work product. If at that time it is determined there has been no significant progress toward meeting the expectations of her job description, we will consider either offering a transfer to another job we feel is better suited to her skills or terminating her employment.

WRITTEN WARNING

Confidential: Personnel matter
Date: April 1, 20xx
Manager:
Regarding employee: Ellie Verbatim
Subject: Organizational skills

I am writing to confirm an important element of the special performance evaluation conducted today. Unfortunately, reports by your supervisor and departmental manager inform me that in the past six weeks, there has been little or no significant improvement in the quality of your work, and we have seen a continued inability to meet deadlines.

We appreciate your dedication to your job and to the organization. We acknowledge your cooperation with the outside consultant we brought in to assist you with organizational skills.

However, with this performance evaluation, as per the employee manual, I am notifying you that I will meet with your supervisor in fifteen days, on April 16, to formally review your work product. If at that time it is determined that there has been no significant progress toward meeting the expectations of your job description, we will consider either offering a transfer to another job we feel is better suited to your skills or terminating your employment.

Tomorrow's a Day Away

Harry Shru never finishes today something he can put off for tomorrow. He is maddeningly consistent in his procrastination, whether it is a matter of making a decision, moving a project along to another stage, or completing an assignment.

Even though he actually meets most final deadlines or goals, his work habits are disruptive to others. His supervisor is unable to conduct midway assessments of projects or to offer any guidance that might steer him toward a more acceptable work product. Coworkers are sometimes unable to complete components of a project on time because they receive no feedback from Harry until the deadline has arrived.

The bottom line is that the organization is less effective, and Harry receives less credit than he might otherwise, because his work is always completed in a mad dash to the finish line.

Verbal Notification

Harry, I've asked you here to discuss your work habits. I'm sure you know that we value you as an employee and appreciate the quality of your work. That has been reflected in your performance evaluations over the years.

However, we would like to see improvement in one particular area. When you are given a major assignment, we would like to see progress reports and samples of the work midway through completion of the task. This will allow us to request changes or make adjustments. At present, although you generally meet deadlines, it has been our experience that there has been no opportunity for feedback during the process.

I'm going to ask you to meet with Connie Bard, your departmental head, and any other supervisors she would like to involve to discuss this. It is our hope that together, you can put in place a process that both improves the quality of your work and allows for your coworkers and supervisors to coordinate your work with others. You should expect to be asked to this meeting within the next week.

Can I answer any questions for you now?

MEMO TO FILE: Noting a request for action

Confidential: Personnel matter
Date: January 15, 20xx
Manager:
Regarding employee: Harry Shru
Subject: Midway progress reports

I met today with Harry Shru to discuss our desire for an improvement in one element of his work habits. I told him that we continue to value him as an employee and appreciate the quality of his work. His recent performance evaluations have included very high ratings and appraisals in most areas.

However, according to his supervisors and department head, although Mr. Shru generally meets deadlines and delivers work of acceptable quality, they are handicapped by his habit of waiting until the very last moment to deliver his reports. He also does not share information about the progress of his work or its contents at waypoints.

I told Mr. Shru that we would like to see progress reports midway, before he has completed a major task, as well as samples of the work. This would allow us to request changes or make adjustments during the process.

I have asked Connie Bard, Mr. Shru's departmental head, to convene a meeting within one business week to discuss this matter; I suggested she might want to include some of Mr. Shru's supervisors. I asked her to put in place a process that both improves the quality of Mr. Shru's work and allows for coworkers and supervisors to coordinate his work with others.

MEMO TO FILE: Offer of assistance

Confidential: Personnel matter
Date: January 18, 20xx
Manager:
Regarding employee: Harry Shru
Subject: Midway progress reports

I received today a memo from Connie Bard in regard to a meeting she held with Harry Shru today. The meeting was held at my request to seek ways to construct a process that improves Mr. Shru's ability to communicate with his supervisors and coworkers about ongoing projects.

I met with Mr. Shru on January 15 to discuss our desire for an improvement in one element of his work habits. I told him that we continue to value him as an employee and appreciate the quality of his work. His recent performance evaluations have included very high ratings and appraisals in most areas.

However, according to his supervisors and department head, although Mr. Shru generally meets deadlines and delivers work of acceptable quality, he is handicapped by his habit of waiting until the very last moment to deliver his reports. He also does not share information about the progress of his work or its contents at waypoints.

Ms. Bard reported that Mr. Shru was very willing to work with her and others in the department to meet their needs. She said that department supervisors suggested that in the future, his assignments be broken down into smaller elements, each with individual deadlines and with interim checkpoints before deadlines. This would allow for validation of the components at various stages, as well as integration of the suggestions and completed work of others in Mr. Shru's projects.

According to Ms. Bard, Mr. Shru agreed fully with the suggestion and promised to work with her and others in the department in this manner.

PERFORMANCE EVALUATION: Acknowledging progress

Confidential: Personnel matter
Date: March 1, 20xx
Manager:
Regarding employee: Harry Shru
Subject: Midway progress reports

I want to commend Mr. Shru on his high level of co-operation with his department head and supervisors in restructuring deadlines on assignments so that there are waypoints before the final deadline. This change came in response to requests from his department that he not wait until the due date for projects before sharing work in progress.

A new set of schedules, put into effect on January 18, breaks projects down into smaller pieces and allows for interim review of work in advance of individual deadlines and before an entire assignment is completed. From all reports, this change in the schedule of assignments has been a very successful adaptation and one that may be useful throughout the organization.

PERFORMANCE EVALUATION: Fails to meet expectations

Confidential: Personnel matter
Date: March 1, 20xx
Manager:
Regarding employee: Harry Shru
Subject: Midway progress reports

I met with Mr. Shru on January 15 to discuss our desire for an improvement in one element of his work habits. I told him that we continue to value him as an employee and appreciate the quality of his work. His recent performance evaluations have included very high ratings and appraisals in most areas.

However, according to his supervisors and department head, although Mr. Shru generally meets deadlines and delivers work of acceptable quality, he is handicapped by his habit of waiting until the very last moment to deliver his reports. He also does not share information about the progress of his work or its contents at waypoints.

In a meeting conducted January 18 by his departmental head, Connie Bard, and including Mr. Shru's supervisors, it was suggested that his assignments be broken down into smaller elements, each with individual deadlines and with interim consultation with team members before deadlines. This would allow for validation of the components at various stages, as well as integration of the suggestions and completed work of others in Mr. Shru's projects.

According to Ms. Bard, Mr. Shru agreed fully with the suggestion and promised to work with her and others in the department in this manner.

However, the change in schedule has not proven to be a success. Mr. Shru continues to delay completion of components of his assignment until the last possible moment. Although he turns in his work by the final deadline specified, he fails to allow supervisors and coworkers to view and comment on projects in progress.

With this evaluation, I am instructing Mr. Shru to meet with Connie Bard within the next week to discuss his work procedure. I am asking for a report on progress by April 1.

It is essential that Mr. Shru find a way to adapt to the requirements of his department in order to meet the specifics of his job description. If Mr. Shru is unable to meet our expectations by April 1, it will be necessary to consider reassignment to another job within the organization or to seek termination of employment.

Confidential: Personnel matter
Date: March 1, 20xx
Manager:
Regarding employee: Harry Shru
Subject: Midway progress reports

I am writing to advise you that we continue to have problems with your refusal to complete job assignments in a timely manner. As we have previously discussed, your practice of waiting until the last possible moment to complete assignments is having an adverse impact on our ability to integrate the work and comments of others and leaves open the possibility that your final work product will not meet our needs.

You were instructed to meet with Connie Bard, your department head, as well as supervisors in your department to come up with schedules that would break down your assignments into smaller elements, each with individual deadlines and with interim consultation with team members before deadlines. This would allow for validation of the components at various stages, and integration of the suggestions and completed work of others into your various projects.

According to Ms. Bard, you agreed fully with the suggestion and promised to work with her and others in the department in this manner.

However, the change in schedule has not proven to be a success. According to your supervisors and department heads, you continue to delay completion of components of your assignments until the last possible moment. Although you turn in your work by the final deadline specified, your disregard for intermediate checkpoints fails to allow supervisors and coworkers to view and comment on projects in progress.

I have instructed Connie Bard to meet with you within the next week to discuss your work procedure. At that meeting, you can discuss modifications to the schedule, clarification of your job description, or special assistance available from the training office. I am asking for a report on progress by April 1.

It is essential that you find a way to adapt to the requirements of your department in order to meet the specifics of your job description. If you are unable to meet our expectations by April 1, it will be necessary to consider reassignment to another job within the organization or to seek termination of employment.

The Overreacher

Betty Allen means well. She just doesn't know how to say no.

She is always the first to volunteer to lead a new initiative, join a new committee, or add new responsibilities to her portfolio. On the one hand, these are admirable traits. Every organization appreciates enthusiasm and commitment to the mission statement. The problem comes when someone is overambitious and is unable to fulfill promises or deliver work of satisfactory quality.

As a manager, there's a difficult quandary here. It's great to have someone who is always so willing to please, but it's a problem when you have someone who promises more than he or she can deliver.

There's another sort of person who falls into the "yes-man" or "yes-woman" category. It's not such a good thing when an employee agrees to ideas that are not proper or appropriate or smart. It is a downright bad thing to have someone who agrees to all requests then does not follow through to accomplish them.

Verbal Notification

We really appreciate your enthusiasm and your willingness to take on new tasks. But no one can do everything. Sometimes jobs don't get done or are not of the quality we know you can produce.

I want you to understand that nobody is going to think any less of you if your hand is not raised every time we ask for help. We'd like you to concentrate on those areas where you can be most helpful and do your best work.

MEMO TO FILE: Noting a request for action

Confidential: Personnel matter
Date: January 15, 20xx
Manager:
Regarding employee: Betty Allen
Subject: Unfinished projects

I met today with Ms. Allen to discuss a group of unfinished tasks for which she had volunteered. I told her we greatly appreciate her enthusiasm and her willingness to take on new tasks but that she should be more selective in volunteering her time.

I assured her that we would not think less of her or penalize her in any way on her employee evaluation if she were to become more selective in her choice of projects. I asked Ms. Allen and her supervisor, Bill Raitt, to report back to me in March about progress in this area.

MEMO TO FILE: Offer of assistance

Confidential: Personnel matter
Date: January 18, 20xx
Manager:
Regarding employee: Betty Allen
Subject: Unfinished projects

I've asked department head Bill Raitt to meet with Betty Allen in the next week to discuss the best use of Ms. Allen's talents in the workplace. I have separately met with Ms. Allen to discuss a group of unfinished tasks for which she had volunteered. I told her we greatly appreciate her enthusiasm and her willingness to take on new tasks but that she should be more selective in volunteering her time.

I assured her that we would not think less of her or penalize her in any way on her employee evaluation if she were to become more selective in her choice of projects.

With this memo, I am requesting Bill Raitt to report back to me in March about progress in this area.

PERFORMANCE EVALUATION: Acknowledging progress

Confidential: Personnel matter
Date: March 1, 20xx
Manager:
Regarding employee: Betty Allen
Subject: Unfinished projects

Ms. Allen continues to be one of our most capable and enthusiastic employees. She has made great progress in becoming more selective when it comes to volunteering for new assignments and special projects.

PERFORMANCE EVALUATION: Fails to meet expectations

Note
This evaluation falls somewhat short of declaring the employee "fails to meet expectations." Rather, it expresses an ongoing concern about a pattern that can be addressed by supervisors in conjunction with the employee. Sometimes, it must be admitted, failure is a shared responsibility.

Confidential: Personnel matter
Date: March 1, 20xx
Manager:
Regarding employee: Betty Allen
Subject: Unfinished projects

Ms. Allen, one of our most capable and enthusiastic employees, has sometimes taken on more tasks and responsibilities than she is capable of completing in a timely manner. I have asked department head Bill Raitt and supervisors in her department to work more closely with her to help her set priorities on the use of her time and abilities.

We have no intention of blaming Ms. Allen for difficulties in completing a work load that is well beyond the job description for her position. It is up to her managers to ensure that we make the most of her skills without overloading her.

WRITTEN ADVISORY

Confidential: Personnel matter
Date: March 1, 20xx
Manager:
Regarding employee: Betty Allen
Subject: Unfinished projects

I'm writing to keep you informed of conversations I have had with your department head, Bill Raitt, about your workload.

As I've told you on several occasions, we consider you one of our most capable and enthusiastic employees. Unfortunately, there have been times when managers in your department have allowed you to take on too many tasks and responsibilities by yourself.

We want to make the most of your talents and give you every opportunity to succeed. I have asked Bill Raitt to monitor assignments you volunteer for or are given to you to ensure that we together set priorities on the best use of your time and abilities.

Demanding, Yet Vague

Ty Evnor knows what he wants: high productivity, good quality, and attention to the bottom line. His problem, though, is he doesn't know how to get down to specifics.

From the point of view of many of the people who work for him, Mr. Evnor possesses a combination of traits that make their lives very frustrating. He is very demanding and at the same time extremely vague.

This is the sort of situation that is very difficult for all involved: supervisors, subordinates, and Mr. Evnor himself. There is no doubt that he means well, and he does not seem to be in violation of any of the organization's rules or its mission statement. The men and women who work for him like him and want to perform at their best. What we have here is a failure to communicate. There is a great deal of wasted or misdirected effort in his department.

Verbal Notification

I want you to know that we continue to think very highly of you as a staffer and as a manager. I've asked you to meet with me because we have discerned a pattern of problems reported by some of your coworkers and some of the staff you supervise.

In speaking with a number of people in the office, I find that you are well respected for your dedication to the mission statement and our shared goals. They all tell me that you expect very much from them as well as from yourself.

However, a common thread that runs through all the employee evaluations and interviews we have conducted is this: Although you are very demanding of excellence and high productivity, you are also vague in your definition of what it is that you want.

I have asked Mary Snow of the human resources department to meet with you within the next week to discuss various options to help you improve your management skills. This could include personalized coaching and training aimed at helping you develop more specific plans and communicate them better.

Do I have your support in moving in this direction?

MEMO TO FILE: Noting a request for action

Confidential: Personnel matter
Date: January 15, 20xx
Manager:
Regarding employee: Ty Evnor
Subject: Improving communication skills

As the result of a series of recent performance evaluations and interviews with staffers who work with or report to Mr. Evnor, we have discerned a pattern of problems in his communication of project goals and other details of assignments.

In a meeting I held with Mr. Evnor today, I told him that we continue to think very highly of him as a staffer and as a manager. I reported that he was well respected by members of his department for his dedication to the mission statement and our shared goals. However, a common thread that runs through all of the employee evaluations and interviews we have conducted is this: Although Mr. Evnor is very demanding of excellence and high productivity, he is also vague in his definition of what he wants.

I have asked Mary Snow of the human resources department to meet with Mr. Evnor within the next week to discuss various options to help improve his management and communication skills. This could include personalized coaching and training aimed at helping him develop more specific plans and communicate them better.

Mr. Evnor expressed to me his full support for this plan. I have asked Mrs. Snow to report back to me by March 1.

MEMO TO FILE: Offer of assistance

Confidential: Personnel matter
Date: January 18, 20xx
Manager:
Regarding employee: Ty Evnor
Subject: Improving communication skills

Per my request, Mary Snow of the human resources department met with Mr. Evnor today to discuss various options to help him improve his management and communication skills.

Mrs. Snow has suggested we enroll Mr. Evnor in a six-day communications skills class offered by a recognized human resources consultant. The course would be conducted over a six-week period. The company will bear the cost of the training.

According to Mrs. Snow, Mr. Evnor was very receptive to the idea. With this memo, I am authorizing the expenditure for the course. I have asked Mrs. Snow and Mr. Evnor to meet with me at the conclusion of the training to discuss progress.

PERFORMANCE EVALUATION: Acknowledging progress

Confidential: Personnel matter
Date: March 1, 20xx
Manager:
Regarding employee: Ty Evnor
Subject: Improving communication skills

Mr. Evnor has been very cooperative with the human resources department in setting up and taking part in communications skills training. This six-week course, which he has just completed, was aimed at improving Mr. Evnor's management skills, specifically in helping him develop more specific plans and communicate them better to coworkers and those he supervises.

Mr. Evnor reports that the course was very valuable and that he intends to make good use of the techniques discussed in the training.

Confidential: Personnel matter
Date: March 1, 20xx
Manager:
Regarding employee: Ty Evnor
Subject: Improving communication skills

Despite recommendations from myself and from the human resources department, Mr. Evnor declined to take part in the communications skills training we had arranged. The six-week course was intended to improve Mr. Evnor's management skills, specifically in helping him develop more specific plans and communicate them better to coworkers and those he supervises.

Although we did not require Mr. Evnor to take the training course, we strongly recommended that he do so.

With this evaluation, I find it necessary to note that Mr. Evnor is not meeting our expectations when it comes to communicating goals, deadlines, and specific strategies to members of his department. The offer of specialized training for Mr. Evnor remains on the table.

At the time of his next evaluation, in September of this year, we expect to see significant improvement in Mr. Evnor's management and communication skills. If no improvement is noted at that time, we may choose to reassign Mr. Evnor to a nonmanagement position or seek termination of his employment.

Confidential: Personnel matter
Date: March 1, 20xx
Manager:
Regarding employee: Ty Evnor
Subject: Improving communication skills

I am writing to emphasize the most important finding of your just-completed employee evaluation. Although we strongly value your commitment to the organization and your job, we feel that you fail to meet expectations when it comes to communicating goals and strategies to coworkers and staffers you supervise.

In January of this year, you were offered special training on communication strategies. You declined to accept that training.

Between now and September of this year, we expect to see significant improvement in your management and communication skills. The offer of special training is still available.

If no improvement is noted by the time of your next evaluation in September, we may choose to reassign you to a nonmanagement position or to seek termination of your employment.

The Overspender

For Barbara Holmes, the bottom line is . . . well, there is no bottom line.

A fact of business and organizational life is that we all must operate within the general or very specific bounds of budgets and regulations. There are limits, or at least guidelines, on money that can be spent on overtime, consultants, materials, and supplies. State and federal law, as well as bargaining unit contracts, if any are in place, may require that employees be paid overtime or granted compensatory time if they are at work beyond the ordinary number of hours.

Ms. Holmes has shown extraordinary dedication to accomplishing any and all assignments given to her. She has a reputation as the go-to person for projects that need fixes or problems in need of solution.

But whether intentionally or not, Ms. Holmes does not pay attention to costs when it comes to fixing a problem or accomplishing a goal where others have not found success. She spends money like it doesn't matter.

Verbal Notification

I've asked you to meet with me to discuss your recent budget report. As you know, your department spent significantly more than was allocated for the previous quarter. The budget line was set at $1.5 million, including an allowance of $200,000 for overtime and a travel budget of $50,000.

The actual numbers show that the department you manage spent $2.1 million, about 40 percent over budget. Overtime expenditures totaled $500,000, an overage of $300,000. The travel budget was overspent by about $50,000.

I do acknowledge that you sought approval for hiring temporary workers to complete the holiday marketing program. The approved budget deviation was $60,000 over the plan, but the actual spending for temporary workforce was $92,000.

As you know, our mission statement says that the customer is our number-one priority, and all managers and department heads have always been encouraged to do whatever it takes—within reason—to meet the needs of our customers. However, your department head must approve any planned budget exception in advance, and in the case of emergency expenditures you must notify your department head within one business day.

Can you explain why your budget expenditures for the previous quarter were so far over planned amounts?

Is there any assistance we can provide, from my office or from other departments including procurement, accounting, or human resources?

MEMO TO FILE: Noting a request for action

Confidential: Personnel matter
Date: January 15, 20xx
Manager:
Regarding employee: Barbara Holmes
Subject: Budget overspending

I met today with Ms. Holmes to discuss her departmental budget report for the just-concluded fourth quarter. We reviewed the fact that total expenditures were 40 percent above planned amounts. The most significant overage came in labor costs: Overtime expenditures were $300,000 over budget, and an approved budget line for hiring of temporary workers was overspent by $32,000. The departmental travel budget was also exceeded by $50,000.

A copy of the department budget, as planned and as spent, is attached to this memo.

I told Ms. Holmes that we appreciated her dedication to the organization and her attention to deadlines and goals. We discussed the fact that our mission statement says that the customer is our number-one priority, and all managers and department heads have always been encouraged to do whatever it takes—within reason—to meet the needs of customers. However, I reminded Ms. Holmes that a department head must approve any planned budget exception in advance, and in the case of emergency expenditures, the department head must be notified within one business day.

I gave Ms. Holmes the opportunity to explain the overspending in her budget. She said she was surprised at the numbers but said that she had concentrated entirely on meeting her goals and deadlines. She said she understood her job description to mean that she had to deliver all assignments on time and that she had latitude to exceed her budget to satisfy the requirements of her job.

I reiterated to Ms. Holmes our appreciation for her dedication to meeting the needs of customers but explained that we cannot be surprised by expenditures. There must be advance approval for exceptions.

I have set up a meeting for tomorrow, January 16, between Ms. Holmes and a representative of the accounting department to review her budget and to answer any questions about the process for monitoring expenditures during a spending period as well as seeking approval for exceptions to the budget line.

MEMO TO FILE: Offer of assistance

Confidential: Personnel matter
Date: January 15, 20xx
Manager:
Regarding employee: Barbara Holmes
Subject: Budget overspending

I have set up a meeting for tomorrow, January 16, between Ms. Holmes and a representative of the accounting department to review her budget and to answer any questions about the process for monitoring expenditures during a spending period as well as seeking approval for exceptions to the budget line.

I have explained to Ms. Holmes that we appreciate her dedication to the organization and her attention to deadlines and goals. However, I reminded Ms. Holmes that a department head must approve any planned budget exception in advance, and in the case of emergency expenditures, the department head must be notified within one business day.

PERFORMANCE EVALUATION: Acknowledging progress

Confidential: Personnel matter
Date: April 15, 20xx
Manager:
Regarding employee: Barbara Holmes
Subject: Budget overspending

I conducted an extra, brief performance evaluation with Ms. Holmes on this date to review with her the budget reports from the recently completed first fiscal quarter.

The numbers were very close to plan, although some excess expenditures from the fourth quarter of the previous year were posted in this quarter.

Ms. Holmes has demonstrated the ability to pay close attention to the elements of the budget and made good use of the monitoring and reporting tools put in place by the accounting department to help avoid overspending. We expect that she will continue to closely watch spending in her department and will seek advance approval for any deviations from plan.

I have asked the accounting department to flag the budget lines for which Ms. Holmes is responsible so that she receives automated notification by e-mail when spending approaches 75 percent of plan. Further, an account analyst will meet once a month with Ms. Holmes through the end of this year to review monitoring and reports on spending.

PERFORMANCE EVALUATION: Fails to meet expectations

Confidential: Personnel matter
Date: April 15, 20xx
Manager:
Regarding employee: Barbara Holmes
Subject: Budget overspending

I conducted an extra, brief performance evaluation with Ms. Holmes on this date to review with her the budget reports from the recently completed first fiscal quarter.

Unfortunately, Ms. Holmes continues to demonstrate difficulty in staying within the budget. Preliminary reports indicate overspending by 30 percent, a slight improvement over the previous quarter but still significantly above plan.

In a review of her performance in January of this year, attached to this evaluation, I reported that I had explained to Ms. Holmes that we appreciate her dedication to the organization and her attention to deadlines and production goals. However, I reminded Ms. Holmes that a department head must approve any planned budget exception in advance, and in the case of emergency expenditures, the department head must be notified within one business day.

We must reach a point at which all managers stay within their departmental budget, allowing for deviations only with approval.

I have asked the accounting department to assign an account analyst to meet with Ms. Holmes once a week, until further notice, to review spending. Further, the accounting department will flag the budget lines for which Ms. Holmes is responsible so that she receives automated notification by e-mail when spending approaches 75 percent of plan. I have asked the accounting department to send copies of the notification to her departmental heads so that they can become involved in monitoring spending if necessary.

We expect Ms. Holmes to demonstrate the ability to pay close attention to the elements of the budget and make good use of the monitoring and reporting tools put in place by the accounting department to help avoid overspending. We expect that she will continue to closely watch spending in her department, and will seek advance approval for any deviations from plan. I have asked departmental heads to keep me up to date on progress in this area. We will review Ms. Holmes's performance on budget management as needed, and no later than July 15.

If there is a continued failure to meet expectations in this area, we may need to remove management of the budget from Ms. Holmes's job description or seek other alterations to her assignment.

WRITTEN WARNING

Confidential: Personnel matter
Date: June 1, 20xx
Manager:
Regarding employee: Barbara Holmes
Subject: Budget overspending

I am writing to advise you that the accounting department has notified me that you continue to overspend budget lines for your department. This has been a matter of concern for us for more than six months.

We have made a number of attempts to offer you assistance from the accounting department, including automated alerts about spending levels and weekly meetings with an analyst to go over interim spending reports.

As you know, we value your efforts on behalf of the organization. However, if you continue to demonstrate an inability to stay within your budget (including any expansions of the spending levels authorized in advanced by supervisors), we will be forced to make changes to your job description to remove budget responsibility from your assignments. This may result in a reassignment to other tasks, a reduction in pay grade, or a limitation on advancement opportunities.

A Salesman Who Can't Close the Sale

On the one hand, it is pretty easy to judge the performance of a salesperson, regardless of whether she or he is on commission or salary; just add up the number of units or the value of goods sold. However, this does not take into account many of the difficult-to-assess variables in sales.

The star salesperson in the department has held that ranking for years. It's hard to remember the last time she did not have the highest sales numbers, and she has won so many bonuses and free vacations and other spiffs that new rules had to be created to share some of the wealth with other salespeople who are successful but not quite at her level.

At the other end of the sales performance charts is Wake Faible. He knows the product, talks a good game, and shows every sign of trying very hard to succeed. But the numbers tell a sad story: He consistently falls short of sales goals, never achieves bonuses, and if he were to be judged in the harshest of lights, it might be said that he is not earning enough to stay on the payroll.

Before Mr. Faible can be judged, a supervisor needs to answer some of these questions:

- Does the star salesperson have the best client list, built up over years in the business?
- Are all of her sales calls to established and satisfied customers of the organization?
- Has Mr. Faible been given all the cold leads, former customers, and a few clients too small or too demanding to be claimed by other salespeople?
- Is there an experienced and impartial sales executive capable of making an impartial assessment of the work performed by Mr. Faible?
- Is there any training that might be offered to him or other accommodations that might be made to help him improve his rate of sales?
- At the most basic level, are sales goals realistic and achievable by salespeople who are selling the same product to the same mix of customers?

Obviously, the answers to these questions are each highly subjective. Managers have to make certain they are fair to all involved.

Verbal Notification

I've asked you to meet with me to discuss ways in which we might be able to help you boost your sales numbers. As you know, you have fallen short of sales goals for each of the past four quarters.

Your income is based on a draw against expected commissions; since your hiring, you have never earned more than 70 percent of your draw.

Obviously, it is to your benefit and ours that you raise the level of sales. As it stands right now, you are being paid only the minimum draw. We expect our salespeople to earn much more than that, and as you know we also have an escalating scale of bonuses and promotional awards.

You have demonstrated a strong knowledge of our line of products and services. We value you as an employee, and we would not have hired you if we didn't believe you had the capability of selling our services and products.

Is there anything we can do to help you improve your results?

MEMO TO FILE: Noting a request for action

Confidential: Personnel matter
Date: January 15, 20xx
Manager:
Regarding employee: Wake Faible
Subject: Sales performance

I met with Mr. Faible today to discuss his sales performance, which has consistently fallen well below expectations since he was hired twelve months ago.

I told Mr. Faible that we value him as an employee and that we would not have hired him if we didn't believe he had the capability of selling our services and products. He has demonstrated a strong understanding of our products.

At our meeting, Mr. Faible expressed two concerns. First of all, he said he felt our practice of assigning particular salespeople to established accounts had the effect of excluding new hires from the most lucrative accounts. Second, he readily agreed to take my offer of specialized training on lead generation and sales techniques.

I told Mr. Faible that it is our organization's policy that a salesperson "owns" an account that they have either originated or developed over time. We do attempt to funnel promising potential customers to all of our salespeople evenly. I told Mr. Faible that I am convinced that he received a fair chance at new accounts.

I will be contacting the human resources department today to request that they set up a training program that will concentrate on two skills: lead generation and sales practices.

MEMO TO FILE: Offer of assistance

Confidential: Personnel matter
Date: January 18, 20xx
Manager:
Regarding employee: Wake Faible
Subject: Sales performance

Mr. Faible has fallen short of sales goals for each of the past four quarters. I have assured Mr. Faible that we value him as an employee and that we would not have hired him if we didn't believe he had the capability of selling our services and products. He has demonstrated a strong understanding of our products.

At our meeting, Mr. Faible expressed two concerns. First of all, he said he felt our practice of assigning particular salespeople to established accounts had the effect of excluding new hires from the most lucrative accounts. Second, he readily agreed to take my offer of specialized training on lead generation and sales techniques.

I have today asked the human resources department to set up a training program for Mr. Faible that will concentrate on two skills: lead generation and sales practices. I asked for a report when the training begins and for interim reports every two weeks from human resources and his supervisor.

I will meet with Mr. Faible again on April 1 to review his progress.

PERFORMANCE EVALUATION: Acknowledging progress

Confidential: Personnel matter
Date: April 1, 20xx
Manager:
Regarding employee: Wake Faible
Subject: Sales performance

Mr. Faible has been working with great dedication to improve his sales performance, and we have noted a sustained upward trend over the past month. He has taken advantage of a training program set up by the human resources department aimed at aiding him in lead generation and sales practices.

We will meet again with Mr. Faible and his supervisor on or about May 15, 20xx, to review sales figures at that time.

PERFORMANCE EVALUATION: Fails to meet expectations

Confidential: Personnel matter
Date: April 1, 20xx
Manager:
Regarding employee: Wake Faible
Subject: Sales performance

Mr. Faible continues to fall short of sales goals. We have set up a specialized training course concentrating on lead generation and sales practices, under the supervision of the human resources department. However, we have not seen progress toward meeting expectations in sales.

We have made it clear to Mr. Faible that we have great hope for him as a salesperson; we believe he has the capability of selling our services and products.

However, at this point we must consider two possibilities: assigning Mr. Faible to a non-sales position if one is available or terminating his employment. We will meet on May 1 for another assessment. Unless we see a significant and sustained improvement in sales figures, we will make a change at that time.

Confidential: Personnel matter
Date: April 1, 20xx
Manager:
Regarding employee: Wake Faible
Subject: Sales performance

As we discussed today, we are disappointed to find that you continue to fall short of sales goals. We appreciate the fact that you have been a dedicated participant in a specialized training course concentrating on lead generation and sales practices, under the supervision of the human resources department. However, we have not seen progress toward meeting expectations in sales.

We believe you have the capability of selling our services and products, and meeting reasonable sales goals.

However, at this point we must consider two possibilities: assigning you to a non-sales position if one is available or terminating your employment. We will meet on May 1 for another assessment. Unless we see a significant and sustained improvement in sales figures, we will make a change at that time.

Strange Numbers at the Ticket Window

There are a few situations in which one person's sales figures can be directly compared to another. Here's one: You have three sales windows, one next to another, and each of the employees at the counter is selling the same item for the same price and working the same hours. It doesn't matter what the product is, its price, or the type of buyer. The three salespeople should have roughly the same sales figures at the end of the day. Actually, the longer the period analyzed, the more likely the numbers will be very close.

Let's say, in this example, you expect sales of 1,000 units per day. If over a reasonable period of time the three sales counters show results of 1,250, 1,000, and 750, here are some possible reasons for the variance:

- The first salesperson may be exceptional, able to use his or her personality to convince customers to buy more or buy more often.
- The second salesperson may merely be taking orders, not trying very hard to reach a higher sales goal.
- The third salesperson, who is recording income well below average or exceptional levels, may be poorly suited to the job, driving away business.
- Another possibility, alas, is that there may be financial irregularities, ranging from outright theft to inaccurate or inappropriate accounting practices.

Few things are quite this simple, but we're going to construct a scenario that allows for direct comparison: ticket salespeople at the gate of a ballpark. There are three windows, one next to the other. There are three classes of tickets available, priced at $10, $20, and $30. Some people are sensitive to price. If the $10 tickets are gone, they may not be willing to spend more. Similarly, some people may want only the best seats in the house and will decline $10 tickets when the $30 seats are sold out.

Each ticket window has the same access to all of the tickets, and each is staffed for the same number of hours each day. That means each of the windows in each group should sell approximately the same number of tickets each day or week. There may be some minor variations from week to week, but over time the numbers should track regularly.

Our salesperson, Neil Whelan, has occupied the middle window in Group A for the past two years. When he first started, his sales numbers were slightly lower than those of coworkers to his left and right. It's a reasonable assumption that he was a bit slower at processing orders and making change. After a few weeks, though, his numbers rose to a nearly exact average for the three windows in his group. Over the past two months, though, his supervisors have noticed a decline in receipts of about 10 to 20 percent in comparison to his coworkers.

No one wants to make any accusations, but the trend has gone on long enough and is of a significant size to raise questions: Is there a falloff in productivity, or could there possibly be an even more serious problem? This is a situation in which employers must tread carefully. Involve your in-house or outside counsel for advice, and make certain any internal investigations are conducted with the highest level of discretion.

If an audit or other examination of sales figures shows that cash is missing from a ticket drawer or account, or if any other sort of criminal activity is suspected, this is a situation that moves away from the performance evaluation process. Get the lawyers involved.

In the case of Mr. Whelan, we're going to assume the problem—if there is one—is related to a falloff in enthusiasm for the job. If at any point the evidence seems to indicate otherwise, call the lawyers.

Verbal Notification

I've asked you to meet with me to discuss your sales performance. We value you as an employee and want to make sure you have every opportunity for success and advancement.

I do note, though, that your cashbox and credit card receipts for the past two months have dropped by 10 to 20 percent below the average for the other two windows. I have re-examined your job description and your working hours and can identify no reason why, over time, your sales numbers should vary significantly from the other ticket windows.

Is there any particular reason why we have noted a falloff in receipts recently? Is there anything we can do to assist your return to a more normal level?

A WORD *to the* WISE

Listen carefully for problems related to the employee's ability to do the job, and be prepared to offer assistance if appropriate. If you hear something that makes you think there may have been some financial misdeeds or crimes, continue to listen but make no comments. Contact the in-house or outside counsel immediately and follow their instructions.

Confidential: Personnel matter
Date: January 15, 20xx
Manager:
Regarding employee: Neil Whelan
Subject: Sales reconciliation

I met today with Neil Whelan, a salesperson at the arena ticket window, to discuss his recent sales figures. When Mr. Whelan first started two years ago, his sales numbers were slightly lower than those of coworkers to his left and right. After a few weeks of training and with experience, his numbers rose to a nearly exact average for the three windows in his group.

Over the past two months, though, his supervisors have noticed a decline in receipts of about 10 to 20 percent in comparison to his coworkers. I considered Mr. Whelan's job description and his working hours and could identify no reason why, over time, his sales numbers should vary significantly from other ticket windows.

I asked Mr. Whelan if he had any explanation for the falloff in sales. Was there a problem we should be aware of?

Mr. Whelan said he was surprised at the numbers I shared with him. He said that he had made no changes to his procedures. However, he did note that there were two new staff members working on either side of him. We discussed the possibility that the coworkers are being more aggressive in seeking out customers and may be more successful at upselling clients, convincing someone who comes to the window planning to buy a $10 seat to instead pay $20 or $30 for a better location.

I have asked Mr. Whelan to meet with the human resources department within the next week to discuss availability of training that might assist him in boosting his numbers. He agreed to do so.

MEMO TO FILE: Offer of assistance

Confidential: Personnel matter
Date: January 18, 20xx
Manager:
Regarding employee: Neil Whelan
Subject: Sales reconciliation

I have asked the human resources department to set up a training course for Mr. Whelan that will assist him in improving his sales. In a meeting on January 15, we discussed the fact that his supervisors have noticed a decline in receipts of about 10 to 20 percent in comparison to his coworkers.

I told Mr. Whelan that I had re-examined his job description and his working hours and could identify no reason why, over time, his sales numbers should vary significantly from other ticket windows. We discussed the possibility that his coworkers are being more aggressive in seeking out customers and may be more successful at upselling clients.

I have asked the director of training in the human resources department to report back to me within two weeks with the details of assistance they are prepared to offer Mr. Whelan. And I have informed Mr. Whelan that we will meet again on or about March 1 to review his sales numbers.

PERFORMANCE EVALUATION: Acknowledging progress

Confidential: Personnel matter
Date: March 1, 20xx
Manager:
Regarding employee: Neil Whelan
Subject: Sales reconciliation

Mr. Whelan has shown good progress in improving his sales results in recent weeks. His daily and monthly numbers are now at or above the average for others at the ticket window. It is our hope that the training courses Mr. Whelan was offered by the human resources department will continue to assist him in improving his sales.

We will continue to monitor the sales figures for Mr. Whelan on a regular basis, as we do for all employees with his job description.

PERFORMANCE EVALUATION: Fails to meet expectations

Confidential: Personnel matter
Date: March 1, 20xx
Manager:
Regarding employee: Neil Whelan
Subject: Sales reconciliation

Mr. Whelan has failed to demonstrate improvement in his sales results for the month just completed. His daily and monthly numbers continue to be 10 to 20 percent below the average for others at the ticket window.

It had been our hope that the training courses Mr. Whelan was offered by the human resources department would assist him in improving his sales.

With this evaluation, I am scheduling another review for April 1 to examine the sales figures for Mr. Whelan for the month of March. If, at that time, his numbers continue to be significantly below those of his coworkers, we will consider reassignment to a different job, if available, or may seek termination of his employment.

WRITTEN WARNING

Confidential: Personnel matter
Date: March 1, 20xx
Manager:
Regarding employee: Neil Whelan
Subject: Sales reconciliation

I am writing to review our conversation of earlier today. As we discussed, you have failed to demonstrate improvement in sales results for the month just completed. Your daily and monthly numbers continue to be 10 to 20 percent below the average for others at the ticket window.

It had been our hope that the training courses offered to you by the human resources department would assist you in improving your sales.

With this evaluation, I am scheduling another review for April 1 to examine the sales figures for the month of March. At that time, if your numbers continue to be significantly below those of your coworkers, we will consider reassignment to a different job, if available, or may seek termination of your employment.

Slow Hand

Production and shipping tasks are mostly automated jobs. Employees are primarily tasked with monitoring computerized manufacturing or packing processes and dealing with "traffic"—the physical movement of product out the door.

It is reasonable to assume that any properly trained worker should be able to reach and sustain a realistic level of production or shipping. The definitions of "reasonable" and "realistic" are, of course, open to some interpretation, but as with most other elements of employment, the most important component of a rule is that it be equitably applied to all workers.

Mickey Clapton, though, is simply slow. He shows up on time, stays at his workstation for his assigned schedule, and otherwise follows all of the elements of his job description. The human resources department and his supervisors are not aware of any disability that might be the cause of his low productivity.

Verbal Notification

I've asked you to meet with me today to discuss some concerns about your productivity on the job. First of all, I want you to understand that we value you as an employee and want to do everything we can to ensure your success here.

However, according to your supervisors and our automated monitoring software, your daily and weekly productivity in the shipping department is significantly below our targets and the average numbers for other workers in the same job classification.

We believe we have done everything we can to establish a safe workplace and enable a high level of productivity. Is there some reason why you are working at a slower pace than others?

Is there anything we can consider doing to make it easier for you to meet the goals we have set?

MEMO TO FILE: Noting a request for action

Confidential: Personnel matter
Date: January 15, 20xx
Manager:
Regarding employee: Mickey Clapton
Subject: Productivity goals

I met with Mr. Clapton today to discuss concerns about his level of productivity. I assured him that we value him as an employee and want to do everything we can to ensure his success here.

However, according to his supervisors and reports generated by our automated monitoring software, Mr. Clapton's daily and weekly productivity in the shipping department is significantly below our targets and the average numbers for other workers in the same job classification.

We believe we have done everything we can to establish a safe workplace and enable a high level of productivity.

I asked Mr. Clapton if there was a reason why he was working at a slower pace than others. He told me that he felt that the chair at his workstation was not of the proper height for him, requiring him to stand up for certain operations; it was also causing him backaches. He said that the problem had not yet risen to the point where it was a medical concern, but he felt it was reducing his productivity and requiring him to take extra time for rest breaks.

I suggested that there might be more ergonomically appropriate furniture available. With this memo, I am requesting the procurement department and the human resources department to meet with Mr. Clapton within the next week to discuss the situation and seek a solution if possible.

MEMO TO FILE: Offer of assistance

Confidential: Personnel matter
Date: January 18, 20xx
Manager:
Regarding employee: Mickey Clapton
Subject: Productivity goals

According to his supervisors and reports generated by our automated monitoring software, Mr. Clapton's daily and weekly productivity in the shipping department is significantly below our targets and the average numbers for other workers in the same job classification.

We believe we have done everything we can to establish a safe workplace and enable a high level of productivity. However, Mr. Clapton told me that he felt that the chair at his workstation was not of the proper height for him, requiring him to stand up for certain operations; it was also causing him backaches. He said that the problem had not yet risen to the point where it was a medical concern, but he felt it was reducing his productivity and requiring him to take extra time for rest breaks.

I have just received a recommendation from the human resources department, after consultation with the procurement department, that we seek more ergonomically appropriate furniture for Mr. Clapton. Human resources also advised that we offer the same sort of accommodation to any other employee performing the same sort of task on the production and shipping line.

I was also advised that several office furniture companies offer samples of their equipment for test periods before purchase. With this memo, I am approving such an arrangement. Mr. Clapton has agreed to test the equipment and provide regular reports to the procurement department over the thirty-day loan period. We are hopeful that a change in furniture for Mr. Clapton will help him boost his productivity.

We will review this matter again on February 15.

PERFORMANCE EVALUATION: Acknowledging progress

Confidential: Personnel matter
Date: February 15, 20xx
Manager:
Regarding employee: Mickey Clapton
Subject: Productivity goals

In January of this year, I met with Mr. Clapton to discuss reports from his supervisors and statistical analysis generated by our automated monitoring software that indicated Mr. Clapton's daily and weekly productivity in the shipping department was significantly below our targets and the average numbers for other workers in the same job classification.

At that time, I requested the procurement department and the human resources department to meet with Mr. Clapton and with outside suppliers to see if there was any available furniture or other equipment that might help boost productivity.

According to Mr. Clapton and his departmental supervisor, a test of new ergonomically specific furniture for the shipping department has resulted in a boost in productivity. We are pleased with this outcome and thank Mr. Clapton for his assistance in evaluating several models of furniture for his workstation.

We will offer the new equipment to any worker performing the same or similar tasks.

Confidential: Personnel matter
Date: February 15, 20xx
Manager:
Regarding employee: Mickey Clapton
Subject: Productivity goals

In January of this year, I met with Mr. Clapton to discuss reports from his supervisors and statistical analysis generated by our automated monitoring software that indicated Mr. Clapton's daily and weekly productivity in the shipping department was significantly below our targets and the average numbers for other workers in the same job classification.

At that time, I requested the procurement department and the human resources department to meet with Mr. Clapton and with outside suppliers to see if there was any available furniture or other equipment that might help boost productivity.

An analysis by an ergonomic consultant engaged by the procurement department reports that there is no advantage to a change in furniture at workstations in the shipping department. Many of the tasks require the worker to stand, and the remainder can be accomplished with the use of standard computer desks and workstations.

At this time, we must consider whether Mr. Clapton is capable of meeting our goals. If improvement is not noted within the next thirty days, we will consider reassignment to another job, if one is available and suitable, or termination from employment.

WRITTEN WARNING

Confidential: Personnel matter
Date: February 15, 20xx
Manager:
Regarding employee: Mickey Clapton
Subject: Productivity goals

In January of this year, I met with you to discuss reports from your supervisors and statistical analysis generated by our automated monitoring software that indicated your daily and weekly productivity in the shipping department was significantly below our targets and the average numbers for other workers in the same job classification.

At that time, I requested the procurement department and the human resources department to meet with you and with outside suppliers to see if there was any available furniture or other equipment that might help boost productivity.

An analysis by an ergonomic consultant engaged by the procurement department reports that there is no advantage to a change in furniture at workstations in the shipping department. Many of the tasks require workers in that job description to stand, and the remainder can be accomplished with the use of standard computer desks and workstations.

At this time, we must consider whether you are capable of meeting our goals. If improvement is not noted within the next thirty days, we will consider reassignment to another job, if one is available and suitable, or termination from employment.

Customer Disservice

Mary French is supposed to be Miss Fixit. As a customer service representative, her job description calls upon her to do everything within reason to make buyers happy. If an order is late or a shipping mistake is made, it's her job to rectify the situation. If a product is defective, she is supposed to arrange for repairs, replacement, or a refund.

The customer service manual includes a set of very specific rules that must be followed in dealing with complaints. It also grants representatives the right to use their judgment in bending the rules—within reason—in favor of a customer. There is also a specific process to follow when a customer service representative or a customer wants to escalate the process to a supervisor for special accommodation.

Miss French sometimes overlooks the "within reason" part of the pledge to serve the customer. On more than a few occasions she has authorized a refund when a repair would have been more appropriate, and she has granted substantial upgrades in service or product to calm an upset customer. No one faults her best intentions, but the end result is a significant deviation from budget plans.

Verbal Notification

I've asked you to meet with me to discuss some of your recent interactions with customers. I want to make it clear that we very much value you as an employee and appreciate your efforts as a customer service representative.

Your job description calls upon you to do everything within reason to make buyers happy. If an order is late or a shipping mistake is made, it's your primary assignment to rectify the situation. If a product is defective, you are supposed to arrange for repairs, replacement, or a refund.

My concern is that from time to time you go beyond the very specific rules that are in the customer service manual. In each case, it is obvious to your supervisors and to me that you have done so with the best of intentions. However, the manual says that although representatives are given some latitude in bending the rules within reason, there is a specific process to follow when a customer service representative or a customer wants to escalate the process to a supervisor for special accommodation.

I'm asking you to take one extra step in the future. If you feel the need to go beyond the ordinary steps we take to accommodate the customer, please follow the rules and seek approval from a supervisor. I expect that in most cases your decisions will be supported, but we need to maintain a process that is intended to keep budget lines within planned levels.

I'd like you to meet with your department head within the next week to review the process for seeking exceptions to established customer service remedies.

MEMO TO FILE: Noting a request for action

Confidential: Personnel matter
Date: January 15, 20xx
Manager:
Regarding employee: Mary French
Subject: Customer service process

I met today with Miss French to discuss some of her recent interactions with customers. I told her at the start of the meeting that I wanted to make it clear that we very much value her as an employee and appreciate her efforts as a customer service representative.

I expressed to her our concern that from time to time in recent months she has gone beyond the very specific rules that are in the customer service manual. In each case, it is obvious to her supervisors and to me that she did so with the best of intentions. However, the manual says that although representatives are given some latitude in bending the rules within reason, there is a specific process to follow when a customer service representative or a customer wants to escalate the process to a supervisor for special accommodation.

In our meeting, I found Miss French to be very cooperative and committed to serving our customers. She told me that she thought her decisions had been proper and fell within the "reasonable" leeway that was a part of her job description.

We agreed that what we were talking about was a judgment call, and I reiterated that we were not questioning her decisions but rather the fact that her supervisors were not kept updated on exceptions to the budget.

I asked Miss French to take one extra step in the future. If she feels the need to go beyond the ordinary steps we take to accommodate the customer, she should seek advance approval from a supervisor. I told her I expected that in most cases her decisions would be supported, but we need to maintain a process that is intended to keep budget lines within planned levels.

Finally, I asked her to meet with her department head within the next week to review the process for seeking exceptions to established customer service remedies.

MEMO TO FILE: Offer of assistance

Confidential: Personnel matter
Date: January 15, 20xx
Manager:
Regarding employee: Mary French
Subject: Customer service process

I met today with Miss French to discuss some of her recent interactions with customers. I told her at the start of the meeting that I wanted to make it clear that we very much value her as an employee and appreciate her efforts as a customer service representative.

I expressed to her the concern that from time to time in recent months she has gone beyond the very specific rules that are in the customer service manual. In each case, it is obvious to her supervisors and to me that she did so with the best of intentions. However, the manual says that although representatives are given some latitude in bending the rules within reason, there is a specific process to follow when a customer service representative or a customer wants to escalate the process to a supervisor for special accommodation.

I have asked Miss French to meet with her department head within the next week to review the process for seeking exceptions to established customer service remedies.

PERFORMANCE EVALUATION: Acknowledging progress

Confidential: Personnel matter
Date: March 1, 20xx
Manager:
Regarding employee: Mary French
Subject: Customer service process

I met with Miss French in January to discuss some of her recent interactions with customers.

I expressed to her the concern that from time to time in recent months she has gone beyond the very specific rules that are in the customer service manual. In each case, it is obvious to her supervisors and to me that she did so with the best of intentions.

I asked Miss French to meet with her department head to review the process for seeking exceptions to established customer service remedies. That meeting took place, and her supervisor informs me that Miss French has very appropriately followed customer service rules since then. Miss French has demonstrated full cooperation with our request that she seek prior approval from a supervisor before going beyond established remedies for customer complaints.

PERFORMANCE EVALUATION: Fails to meet expectations

Confidential: Personnel matter
Date: March 1, 20xx
Manager:
Regarding employee: Mary French
Subject: Customer service process

I met with Miss French in January to discuss some of her recent interactions with customers. I told her at the start of the meeting that I wanted to make it clear that we very much value her as an employee and appreciate her efforts as a customer service representative.

I expressed to her the concern that from time to time in recent months she has gone beyond the very specific rules that are in the customer service manual. In each case, it is obvious to her supervisors and to me that she did so with the best of intentions.

I asked Miss French to meet with her department head to review the process of seeking exceptions to established customer service remedies. That meeting took place.

I am informed, though, that Miss French has continued to go beyond the specific remedies that are allowed in her job description. On several occasions, for example, she has permitted a full refund to a customer rather than authorizing a repair. The manual says refunds are to be offered only in the first thirty days after a product has been delivered.

With this memo, I am directing Miss French to meet with her department head and with a representative of the human resources department within ten days to once again review the rules for her job description. I will seek a report from her department head on April 1 to inform me whether this issue has been resolved or whether it continues.

If Miss French fails to demonstrate an ability to follow the rules, we will at that time consider either a reassignment to a different job, if available, or termination from employment.

Confidential: Personnel matter
Date: March 1, 20xx
Manager:
Regarding employee: Mary French
Subject: Customer service process

I am informed by your supervisors that you continue to go beyond the specific remedies allowed in your job description. On several occasions, you have permitted a full refund to a customer rather than authorizing a repair. The manual says that refunds are to be offered only in the first thirty days after a product has been delivered.

I have made it clear to you on several occasions that we very much value you as an employee and appreciate your efforts as a customer service representative. However, we cannot permit unauthorized expenditures that go beyond budget lines.

With this memo, I am directing you to meet with your department head within ten days to once again review the rules for your job description. A representative of the human resources department will also attend.

I will seek a report from your department head on April 1 to inform me whether this issue has been resolved or whether it continues.

We have every hope that you will adjust your practices to meet the rules of your job. However, if you fail to demonstrate an ability to consistently follow the rules, we will at that time consider either a reassignment to a different job, if available, or termination from employment.

Chapter 3

DISORGANIZATION AND INEFFICIENCY

THERE IS AN oft-used simile in business and technology that describes the difficulty of quantifying something that is qualitative: "It's like nailing Jell-O to the wall."

That sort of very difficult task is exactly what managers face when they have to evaluate the performance of workers whose job description does not involve production of a specific amount of units, response to a particular number of repair calls, or development of a stated amount of pages, cases, referrals, payments, bills, or other physical things.

For example, how do you evaluate a customer service representative whose principal job task is to "keep the clients happy"? What is the measure of efficiency of a receptionist? How can you judge the work of a custodian? What is the proper way to assess the quality of work of an artist or a Web designer?

One answer is, as best you can, to "freeze the Jell-O." By that we mean, look for as many ways as possible to quantify or assess the quality of work in a fair and equitable manner that applies to all workers in a particular job.

There are several ways to do this. Conduct surveys of customers about the quality of service they received in response to their calls or letters. Do the same with visitors who meet the receptionist, and establish benchmarks for specific levels of cleanliness or determine reasonable targets for specific custodial tasks.

The Company Mess

The first person any visitor sees when they enter the door is Mary Stuart, the friendly and welcoming receptionist. They're also likely to see a half-eaten sandwich on the counter, a pile of unsorted magazines and other papers, and sometimes a stack of confidential internal memos and documents that are there for the perusal of any passersby.

Where to begin? The front desk should present a great first impression to any visitor or client. There is specific language in the employee manual that prohibits eating, drinking, or smoking anywhere other than in designated locations: the employee lounge, the break room, or in a designated area of the parking lot out of view of the public. Internal memos and documents, including personnel matters, wholesale price lists, and organizational matters are required to be kept in designated places including secure drawers, file cabinets, or other places that are out of view of persons without permission to see them.

Verbal Notification

Mary, I've asked you to meet with me to discuss your management of the front desk. We are concerned that you are not presenting a clean and organized appearance to visitors.

On a number of occasions in the past month, we have noticed internal memos and documents in plain view on your desk. These materials are not meant to be disclosed to visitors and clients. You have also made it a general practice to eat your lunch at your desk, which does not present a professional appearance to visitors.

We value you as an employee and hope for your future success in the organization. However, we must insist that you fully follow your job description and the employee manual. I'd like to go over a few of the pertinent elements of the job description with you now.

MEMO TO FILE: Noting a request for action

Confidential: Personnel matter
Date: January 15, 20xx
Manager:
Regarding employee: Mary Stuart
Subject: Personal conduct

I met with Ms. Stuart this morning to discuss her management of the front desk. I told her we were concerned that she was not presenting a clean and organized appearance to visitors.

I reported that on a number of occasions in the past month, various supervisors and executives have noticed internal memos and documents in plain view on her desk. I reiterated to Ms. Stuart that these materials are not meant to be disclosed to visitors and clients.

We also discussed the fact that Ms. Stuart has also made it a general practice to eat lunch at her desk, which does not present a professional appearance to visitors.

I told Ms. Stuart that we value her as an employee and hope for her future success in the organization. However, we must insist that she fully follow her job description and the employee manual. I reviewed with her several of the pertinent elements of the job description.

In response, Ms. Stuart said that she felt that she was not being offered full support in her job. For example, she said, the front desk does not have sufficient filing space to hold company-confidential memos and files that she was supposed to read during the course of the day. She said she has asked her supervisor for additional office furniture several times, but none has been provided.

As far as lunch, Ms. Stuart said, she felt that this was an improper criticism. She said that for three or four days out of the week the scheduled relief receptionist was given other assignments that prevented her from filling in at the front desk during the lunch break. As a result, Ms. Stuart said she had a choice between leaving the front desk unstaffed—in violation of her job description—or working through her own lunch period and eating at her desk.

I told Ms. Stuart I would look into the situation and meet with her again within a week.

MEMO TO FILE: Offer of assistance

Confidential: Personnel matter
Date: January 18, 20xx
Manager:
Regarding employee: Mary Stuart
Subject: Personal conduct

I have found that Ms. Stuart's explanation for reports that she was not presenting a clean and organized appearance to visitors to be accurate. Her workspace does not include proper filing furniture to hold the company's confidential memos and documents. It is also apparent that other departments are not providing lunch-hour relief staff on a regular basis.

I met today again with Ms. Stuart to inform her that I have instructed the office services department to immediately provide a lockable file cabinet to sit beneath her desk and asked her to keep all documents in the cabinet when not in use. At times when she is reading memos or filling out necessary reports, she is to move them into a folder on her desk any time visitors are in the lobby.

I also advised her that I have directed department heads to make sure that a relief receptionist is dispatched to the lobby every day at noon. If there is a problem with staffing the reception desk, I asked Ms. Stuart to call the human resources department and inform them immediately.

I thanked Ms. Stuart for her work and told her that we would meet again in one month to review the situation.

PERFORMANCE EVALUATION: Acknowledging progress

Confidential: Personnel matter
Date: March 15, 20xx
Manager:
Regarding employee: Mary Stuart
Subject: Personal conduct

In the past month, Ms. Stuart has greatly improved her performance as front-desk receptionist.

Her workstation, now equipped with proper filing cabinets and folders, has permitted her to file away company-confidential memos and documents so that they are not in public view.

Ms. Stuart reports that she is now able to leave her desk every day to have lunch in the break room or out of the building because a lunch-hour relief staffer arrives daily on schedule.

PERFORMANCE EVALUATION: Fails to meet expectations

Confidential: Personnel matter
Date: April 1, 20xx
Manager:
Regarding employee: Mary Stuart
Subject: Personal conduct

Despite the provision of proper filing cabinets and folders at the front desk, Ms. Stuart continues to fail to meet expectations for her job description. Supervisors report they regularly see company-confidential memos and documents in public view on the desktop.

With this memo, I am informing Ms. Stuart that we expect her to immediately follow all company regulations and the elements of her job description and to keep all such papers out of sight. We will review this situation again in fifteen days. If we do not note a significant improvement at that time, we may choose to reassign Ms. Stuart to a new job or seek her immediate termination from employment.

Confidential: Personnel matter
Date: April 1, 20xx
Manager:
Regarding employee: Mary Stuart
Subject: Personal conduct

I am writing to inform you that we have determined that you continue to fail to meet expectations for your job description as a front-desk receptionist.

Despite the provision of proper filing cabinets and folders at the front desk, we have found that you continue to leave company-confidential memos and documents in public view on the desktop.

With this memo, I am informing you that we expect you to immediately follow all company regulations and the elements of your job description and to keep all such papers out of sight. We will review this situation again in fifteen days. If we do not note a significant improvement at that time, we may choose to reassign you to a new job or seek your immediate termination from employment.

A Tangled Web

In today's world, the first (and perhaps the most important) impression most clients or would-be customers have of an organization is the organization's public Web site. For the majority of existing or potential clients, it's an automatic assumption that they can find out about products, services, or make contact with members of the staff through a Web site with an obvious name. (We all assume that the Acme Explosives Company can be reached through *www.acmeexplosives.com* or something equally simple to find. Just ask valued customer W. E. Coyote.)

Once we arrive at a page, we expect to see an attractive, orderly presentation. All the links should work, there should be a logical organization to the pages, and complex sites should include a quick and simple search function.

However, this is obviously an area where Jell-O is being applied to the wall. One of the problems faced by writers, artists, and designers is that once they are deep into a project, they know exactly what they mean to say, even though others may not comprehend it when they see it.

That is apparently the situation with Marybeth Adams, a talented artist who fills her cubicle with handsome line drawings and paintings but has filled the organization's Web site with a confusing mix of disorganized elements, broken links, and useless or outdated information. It all makes sense to her, she says, but comments from customers and staffers say otherwise.

Verbal Notification

I've asked you to meet with me today to discuss the design and functionality of the company Web site, a core element of your job description.

We feel the Web site is not meeting our needs. Although it is very attractive, we find that it is not kept up to date with our latest products and services, and many of the links to information appear to be broken or out of date.

We value you as an employee and hope you will have success in all of your efforts. However, we do consider the organizational Web site to be a core piece of our communication with existing and prospective customers, and we want to see an immediate, substantial improvement.

Is there anything we can do to assist you in meeting our expectations?

MEMO TO FILE: Noting a request for action

Confidential: Personnel matter
Date: January 15, 20xx
Manager:
Regarding employee: Marybeth Adams
Subject: Web site management

I met today with Ms. Adams to discuss the design and functionality of the company Web site, a core element of her job description.

I told her we feel the Web site is not meeting our needs. Although it is very attractive, we find that it is not kept up to date with our latest products and services and many of the links to information appear to be broken or out of date.

I assured Ms. Adams that we value her as an employee and hope she will have success in all of her efforts. However, we do consider the organizational Web site to be a core piece of our communication with existing and prospective customers, and we want to see an immediate, substantial improvement.

I asked Ms. Adams if there was anything we could do to assist her in meeting our expectations. She responded that she felt that although she was a capable artist, she had never received proper training in the development and maintenance of a Web site. Further, she said, the computer hardware and software provided to her were the same as those provided to clerical staffers and did not include appropriate facilities for computer-based design and Web site work.

With this memo, I am directing:

- The human resources department to meet with Ms. Adams within five days to discuss development of a training program for Web site development and maintenance. It appears we will need to engage the services of an outside consultant or training company for this purpose, and I will support necessary expenditures for this purpose.
- The office services department to meet with Ms. Adams within five days to produce hardware and software specifications for a graphics workstation appropriate for Web site development. I will approve necessary expenditures for this purpose.

I have asked Ms. Adams to meet with me again on March 1 to discuss progress in this area.

MEMO TO FILE: Offer of assistance

Confidential: Personnel matter
Date: January 18, 20xx
Manager:
Regarding employee: Marybeth Adams
Subject: Web site management

I have received paperwork from the human resources and the office services departments in regard to assisting Ms. Adams in performing her duties in improving the organization's Web site. I fully outlined our expectations in a memo to file dated January 15, 20xx.

The human resources department has recommended we engage an outside consultant, for a period of ten days, to work directly with Ms. Adams and train her on the use of current Web development and information management systems. They have identified an appropriate consultant. I have approved their request, with one proviso: I will ask the office services department to have new computer hardware and software equipment in place before the training begins.

The office services department has recommended purchase of a new computer, equipped with current software, for the purposes of development and maintenance of an organizational Web site. Further, they recommend that the in-house computer services department provide a dedicated high-speed broadband communication link that will better support Ms. Adams in the performance of her job. I will approve necessary expenditures for this purpose.

As previously noted, I have asked Ms. Adams to meet again with me on March 1 to review progress in this matter.

PERFORMANCE EVALUATION: Acknowledging progress

Confidential: Personnel matter
Date: March 1, 20xx
Manager:
Regarding employee: Marybeth Adams
Subject: Web site management

I want to note the significant progress Ms. Adams has made in improving the appearance, functionality, and inherent value of the organization's Web site. There are still improvements we expect to be made. A memo from Ms. Adams describing her work in progress is attached to this evaluation.

Ms. Adams has made excellent use of the new computer hardware and software provided to her by the office services department. According to the human resources department, Ms. Adams received intensive training by an outside consultant on the use of the hardware and software.

I have asked for another review of progress on April 1.

PERFORMANCE EVALUATION: Fails to meet expectations

Confidential: Personnel matter
Date: March 1, 20xx
Manager:
Regarding employee: Marybeth Adams
Subject: Web site management

Although we have made significant efforts to improve her training and computer equipment, Ms. Adams continues to fail to meet our expectations in developing and maintaining our organizational Web site.

As directed by me on January 18, Ms. Adams was provided with new computer hardware and graphics software. She was also given intensive training by an outside consultant on the use of the hardware and software.

At this point, we consider the functionality and inherent value of the Web site to be below acceptable quality. Information is out of date, links are incomplete or broken, and the design is confusing.

With this memo, I am informing Ms. Adams that we will review this situation again in fifteen days. If we do not note a significant improvement at that time, we may choose to reassign Ms. Adams to a new job or seek her immediate termination from employment.

Confidential: Personnel matter
Date: March 1, 20xx
Manager:
Regarding employee: Marybeth Adams
Subject: Web site management

I am writing to inform you that in our judgment, we find your work on the organization's Web site to be well below our expectations.

Although we have made significant efforts to improve your training and computer equipment, at this point we consider the functionality and inherent value of the Web site to be below acceptable quality. Information is out of date, links are incomplete or broken, and the design is confusing.

We will review this situation again in fifteen days. If we do not note a significant improvement at that time, we may choose to reassign you to a new job or seek your immediate termination from employment.

Cleanup on Aisle Nine

It's a dirty job, but someone has to do it. The break room has a coffee machine, a microwave, and a large refrigerator. It's operated on the honor system. If you put your sandwich in the fridge in the morning, it's supposed to waiting for you at lunch. By the same token, you're not supposed to leave food in the refrigerator for extended periods of time. Everyone is asked to clean up after they use the coffee maker or the microwave. It's all spelled out on signs.

But something is broken in the break room. The microwave regularly builds up a crust of splattered food, the coffeemaker's clear glass carafe is a frightening mix of unnatural colors, and the refrigerator looks like a science experiment gone wrong. To add insult to possible injury, there have been reports of missing brownies.

Chris Post is the night custodian for this part of the building, and though his job description does not specifically state he is to clean up the break room, it does say he is responsible for the maintenance of a clean workplace throughout his assigned area.

Verbal Notification

I've asked you to meet with me today to discuss an element of your job performance. We have received a number of complaints that the break room is not cleaned overnight during the period when you are on duty.

Your job description states that you are responsible for maintaining a clean workplace on the first and second floors, an area that includes the break room.

Is there a reason why the break room is not being cleaned nightly?

MEMO TO FILE: Noting a request for action

Confidential: Personnel matter
Date: January 15, 20xx
Manager:
Regarding employee: Chris Post
Subject: Janitorial duties

I met with Mr. Post today to discuss the fact that we have received a number of complaints that the break room is not cleaned overnight during the period when he is on duty.

I reviewed with him his job description, which states he is responsible for maintaining a clean workplace on the first and second floors, an area that includes the break room.

I asked him if there was a reason why the break room was not being cleaned nightly. Mr. Post said it had been his understanding that the break room was not part of his responsibilities. He referred to the numerous notices on the door and within the break room that call upon all employees to clean up after themselves. He noted that the job description did not make mention of the break room.

In response, I told Mr. Post that although we do ask users of the break room to clean up the area after they have used the microwave, refrigerator, and tables, in the end the ultimate responsibility for cleaning the room lies with the maintenance staff.

To clarify matters, with this memo I am asking the human resources department to amend the job description assigned to Mr. Post to specifically include the break room.

MEMO TO FILE: Offer of assistance

Confidential: Personnel matter
Date: January 18, 20xx
Manager:
Regarding employee: Chris Post
Subject: Janitorial duties

I have received from the human resources department a copy of a revised job description for Mr. Post that specifically includes cleaning the break room. I am also informed that a representative of human resources directed the head of the maintenance department to discuss the amended job description with Mr. Post.

We will review this matter again in fifteen days.

PERFORMANCE EVALUATION: Acknowledging progress

Confidential: Personnel matter
Date: February 6, 20xx
Manager:
Regarding employee: Chris Post
Subject: Janitorial duties

We have noted a marked improvement in the cleanliness of the second-floor break room in the past two weeks and acknowledge the work by Mr. Post in this area.

PERFORMANCE EVALUATION: Fails to meet expectations

Confidential: Personnel matter
Date: February 6, 20xx
Manager:
Regarding employee: Chris Post
Subject: Janitorial duties

We continue to receive complaints about the cleanliness of the second-floor break room. On January 15, I met with Mr. Post to discuss this matter. On January 18, his job description was amended to specifically include the break room as his responsibility.

With this evaluation, I am informing Mr. Post that we will review this situation again in fifteen days. If we do not note a significant improvement at that time, we may choose to reassign Mr. Post to a new job if available or seek his immediate termination from employment.

WRITTEN WARNING

Confidential: Personnel matter
Date: February 6, 20xx
Manager:
Regarding employee: Chris Post
Subject: Janitorial duties

I am writing to inform you that we continue to receive complaints about the cleanliness of the second-floor break room. As you know, I met with you on January 15 to discuss this matter, and on January 18 your job description was amended to specifically include the break room as your responsibility.

With this memo, I am informing you that we will review this situation again in fifteen days. If we do not note a significant improvement at that time, we may choose to reassign you to a new job if available or seek your immediate termination from employment.

Mayonnaise by the Gallon

Who buys those nine-gallon jugs of mayonnaise at the warehouse store? More importantly, does it really make sense to buy that much of a perishable commodity, or would it be a better idea to buy smaller portions?

Along the same lines, is it smart to keep the office-supply closet fully stocked with dozens of boxes of printer toner and fax paper, or is it a better idea not to maintain a prepaid inventory of items that (1) could become un-needed because of changes in equipment, (2) could go stale over time, or (3) could just as easily be ordered on a "just in time" (JIT) basis when needed?

If you've got the time and nothing better to do, ask an accountant or an economist to explain to you the concept of future value. As it applies to inventory, here's the gist: If you pay $10 for something today that you won't need for a year, you need to add to the price the lost earnings you would have made on the money if you had invested it until you actually needed to buy the item.

Some items go down in price over time. A good example is most high-tech electronics. It generally does not make sense to stockpile boxes of computers a year before they are needed because history has shown that prices tend to go down and capabilities go up with each new generation of technology.

On the other hand, some prices tend to rise over time. Almost anything that involves labor tends to cost more as wages rise. So, for example, it might make sense to lock in an hourly rate for lawn mowing or snowplowing . . . if you aren't worried about a future lack of rain or snow.

Then there are items that fluctuate wildly. Relatively few people can consistently predict the prices of commodities, from oil and gasoline to crops and paper goods. (If you can figure out a trend, get a job as a trader. Buy low and sell high, or sell high and hope you can buy low to fulfill a future contract.)

This all brings us to Jackson Tandy, inventory manager. He's one of the company's senior employees, with nearly thirty years on the job. He knows the organization and its need for supplies as well as anyone, and he's a very capable, diligent manager of the supply room. There's almost no doubt that if you need staples, envelopes, or pens, he's got them waiting. He's applied the same one-stop-shopping scheme to technology, too. If a computer keyboard or a monitor fails, he's got a replacement ready.

But here's the bad news: The contents of his supply room represents several hundred thousand dollars of product that may not be needed for months or years and may never be needed. That was okay under the old way of doing business, but not any more. For several years he has been asked to reduce the inventory and work with outside vendors to provide JIT . . . but he doesn't seem to get it.

Verbal Notification

I've asked you to meet with me to discuss your procurement practices.

First of all, I want you to know that we value you as a long-time employee and hope for your success in the future. However, we are concerned about what we see as wasteful practices.

For the past several years, all departments in the organization have been asked to make every effort to reduce the amount of inventory of supplies to the absolute minimum. With modern computer-based tools, we have determined that we are better off buying smaller quantities of supplies when needed—even if the per-unit price is higher—instead of maintaining large stocks that may never be used or may spoil over time.

I realize that this represents a significant change from the way we made purchases when you first joined the organization. However, management practices do change over time. Just as one example, we have found that it does not make economic sense for us to stockpile computer equipment in case of failure of a component. For one thing, technology is changing so fast that equipment that is stored for months or years may be completely outdated by the time it is put into service. At the same time, prices for new computer equipment have been on a steady decline for many years.

I would like to have you meet with the human resources department to schedule a one-day training session with a procurement expert.

MEMO TO FILE: Noting a request for action

Confidential: Personnel matter
Date: January 15, 20xx
Manager:
Regarding employee: Jackson Tandy
Subject: Procurement practices

I met today with Mr. Tandy to discuss his procurement practices.

For the past several years, all departments in the organization have been asked to make every effort to reduce the amount of inventory of supplies to the absolute minimum. With modern computer-based tools, we have determined that we are better off buying smaller quantities of supplies when needed—even if the per-unit price is higher—instead of maintaining large stocks that may never be used or may spoil over time.

I told Mr. Tandy that we value him as a long-time employee and hope for his success in the future. However, we are concerned about what we see as wasteful practices.

I discussed with Mr. Tandy the fact that we are aware that this represents a significant change from the way we made purchases when he first joined the organization. However, I explained, management practices do change over time.

I cited as one example the fact that we have found it does not make economic sense to stockpile computer equipment in case of failure of a component. Technology is changing so fast that equipment that is stored for months or years may be completely outdated by the time it is put into service. At the same time, prices for new computer equipment have been on a steady decline for many years.

I asked Mr. Tandy to meet with the human resources department to schedule a one-day training session with a procurement expert. He agreed to do so.

MEMO TO FILE: Offer of assistance

Confidential: Personnel matter
Date: January 18, 20xx
Manager:
Regarding employee: Jackson Tandy
Subject: Procurement practices

I am informed by the human resources department that they have engaged the services of a procurement consultant to meet with Mr. Tandy within the next week to assist him in developing a new "just-in-time" purchasing program.

I have asked for a review of the status of Mr. Tandy's job performance on March 1.

PERFORMANCE EVALUATION: Acknowledging progress

Confidential: Personnel matter
Date: March 1, 20xx
Manager:
Regarding employee: Jackson Tandy
Subject: Procurement practices

The accounting department informs me that Mr. Tandy has met their expectations in redesigning the procurement program for office supplies. Mr. Tandy received special training from a procurement consultant in January.

Confidential: Personnel matter
Date: March 1, 20xx
Manager:
Regarding employee: Jackson Tandy
Subject: Procurement practices

According to an audit by the accounting department, the office supply bureau run by Mr. Tandy continues to make purchases of large quantities of items and to maintain an inventory of supplies well in excess of the short-term needs of the organization.

I met with Mr. Tandy on January 15 to discuss his procurement practices, and on January 18 the human resources department hired a consultant to assist him in revamping purchasing practices to a "just-in-time" model.

I have assured Mr. Tandy that we value him as a long-time employee and hope for his success in the future. However, in recent weeks and months he has been failing to meet expectations in the fulfillment of his job assignment.

With this evaluation, I am informing Mr. Tandy that we will review this situation again in fifteen days. If we do not note a significant improvement at that time, we may choose to reassign Mr. Tandy to a new job if available or seek his immediate termination from employment.

Confidential: Personnel matter
Date: March 1, 20xx
Manager:
Regarding employee: Jackson Tandy

I am writing to inform you that according to an audit by the accounting department, the office supply bureau continues to make purchases of large quantities of items and to maintain an inventory of supplies well in excess of the short-term needs of the organization.

I met with you on January 15 to discuss your procurement practices, and on January 18 the human resources department hired a consultant to assist you in revamping purchasing practices to a "just-in-time" model.

We value your service as a long-time employee and hope for your success in the future. However, in recent weeks and months you have been failing to meet expectations in the fulfillment of your job assignment.

With this evaluation, I am informing you that we will review this situation again in fifteen days. If we do not note a significant improvement at that time, we may choose to reassign you to an appropriate new job if available or seek your immediate termination from employment.

Chapter 4

EDUCATION AND TRAINING

TEMPUS FUGIT—TIME FLIES, and things change. In the separate and now merged careers of the two authors of this book, we began with manual typewriters, rotary dial telephones, libraries paneled with printed (and very outdated) reference books, and huge rooms full of filing cabinets (stocked with yellowing carbon copies and handwritten ledgers.)

Today, of course, we live in a world of personal computers, tiny cell phones, the amazing, expanding, and ever-evolving Internet (Google me the following . . .), and with everything tied together in a quick electronic database in which every word, phrase, and concept is indexed and searchable at the click of a mouse. Oh yes, we've got mice, too.

Somewhere out there is a receptionist who has never managed to master the ability to transfer a call to a different extension, an accountant who uses a hand-cranked adding machine, and an office manager who keeps track of hours worked and supplies dispensed in a black-and-white marbled composition book. The rest of us have to keep up with the times—whether we want to or not—with each earthquake of new technology.

Just a decade or so ago, most salespeople were sending their clients a catalog or a brochure or inviting a current or prospective customer to a showroom where products were on display. Today, it's all up on the Internet: product images, pricelists, shopping carts, shipping costs, and the ability to track your order from the assembly line to your loading dock (or mailbox.)

Not all that long ago, there was a class of workers called secretaries and a subclass called the "steno pool." Their job was to sit across the desk from an executive and take dictation in shorthand, and then type their notes in the form of a letter that was signed, folded, and placed in an envelope (with a typewritten address) and placed in the hands of a uniformed representative of the federal government for hand delivery to another office in a few days. Today, well, you get the idea. The executive jots a few notes into an e-mail program or pecks at a few buttons on a cell phone and zaps the message from one desk to another in the office, across town, or around the world in a few milliseconds.

The biggest adjustment some people have had to make in recent years is to the change in the social environment of the workplace. For most of the twentieth century, there was a strict and well-defined hierarchy: The bosses (mostly men, and mostly of a certain background) were locked away upstairs in closed offices fronted by fierce guardians at battleship reception desks. At the other end of the scale, workers were isolated from each other, assigned a small piece of the puzzle to solve by themselves.

The modern workplace began to change with the arrival of the cubicle and all that it presaged: management by consensus and the sharing of responsibilities and rewards. Not everything is perfect, of course, but the concept is pretty widespread—a staff is meant to be a team, not a pecking order.

The Benchwarmer

Theresa Kern keeps things to herself. She's a capable and bright person, but she's not much of a team player. Information is a commodity that she holds very tightly: any progress in a work short of its completion, news from customers and competitors, and any advice she might be able to offer others on how to succeed in business. All this she keeps a deep, dark secret.

Supervisors and managers do not need to know about an employee's personal life, but they do have a reasonable expectation that staffers will keep them informed about projects and offer any other information that will help the organization accomplish its goals.

Verbal Notification

I've asked you to meet with me to discuss our concern that you are not providing us with feedback on projects you have underway and about information you gather that might help others in their own work.

I want you to know that we value you as an employee and hope for your success in the organization. We are generally pleased with the quality of your work. However, we do feel that you do not share enough information with your department about projects in progress or about potential or current clients.

We'd like to work with you to improve your communication skills in the workplace. I would like you to meet with the human resources department tomorrow morning to discuss a training program they will design for you.

Confidential: Personnel matter
Date: January 15, 20xx
Manager:
Regarding employee: Theresa Kern
Subject: Communication skills

I met today with Ms. Kern to discuss our concern that she is not providing us with feedback on projects she has underway and about information she gathers that might help others in their work.

I assured Ms. Kern that we value her as an employee and hope for her success in the organization. I told her we were generally pleased with the quality of her work. However, we do feel that Ms. Kern does not share enough information with her department about projects in progress or about potential or current clients.

I told Ms. Kern that we would like to work with her to improve her communication skills in the workplace. I have asked Ms. Kern to meet with the human resources department tomorrow morning to discuss a training program they will design for her. She agreed to do so.

Confidential: Personnel matter
Date: January 18, 20xx
Manager:
Regarding employee: Theresa Kern
Subject: Communication skills

The human resources department has recommended that we send Ms. Kern to a week-long seminar on communication skills, offered by a local consultancy. The course is aimed at improving Ms. Kern's ability to provide us with feedback on projects she has underway and about information she gathers that might help others in their own work.

Ms. Kern has agreed to take the course, and I have approved payment to the consultants.

I have asked the involved supervisors and the human resources department to report back to me on March 1 to discuss the status of this issue.

PERFORMANCE EVALUATION: Acknowledging progress

Confidential: Personnel matter
Date: March 1, 20xx
Manager:
Regarding employee: Theresa Kern
Subject: Communication skills

Supervisors and the human resources department report that Ms. Kern has demonstrated significant improvement in communication skills in recent weeks.

She completed a seminar set up by the human resources department, and I am informed that her department head and managers are very happy with what they see as a new commitment to keeping them posted on projects in progress and advising them of news from clients.

PERFORMANCE EVALUATION: Fails to meet expectations

Confidential: Personnel matter
Date: March 1, 20xx
Manager:
Regarding employee: Theresa Kern
Subject: Communication skills

Supervisors and the human resources department report that Ms. Kern has failed to demonstrate significant improvement in communication skills in recent weeks.

She completed a seminar set up by the human resources department, but I am informed that her department head and managers report they have not seen any change in what they have reported as a reluctance to keep them posted on projects in progress and advising them of news from clients.

With this evaluation, I am advising Ms. Kern that we will review this situation once more in thirty days. At that time, if we do not see significant improvement in communication skills, we will either consider reassignment to a new position, if one is available and appropriate, or seek immediate termination from employment.

WRITTEN WARNING

Confidential: Personnel matter
Date: March 1, 20xx
Manager:
Regarding employee: Theresa Kern
Subject: Communication skills

I am writing to inform you that your departmental supervisors and the human resources department report that, in their opinion, you have failed to demonstrate significant improvement in communication skills in recent weeks.

You completed a seminar set up by the human resources department, but I am informed that your department head and managers report they have not seen any change in what they have reported as a reluctance to keep them posted on projects in progress and to advise them of news from clients.

I am advising you that we will review this situation once more in thirty days. At that time, if we do not see significant improvement in communication skills, we will either consider reassignment to a new position, if one is available and appropriate, or seek immediate termination from employment.

The Luddite

Jerry Watson rides a bicycle to work, which probably sums him up pretty well. If something has worked for him for twenty years, there's no reason to change. That's the same way he feels about innovation in the workplace. He has made clear his disdain for the computer terminal on his desk, and he has refused to transfer the scribbled appointments from his desktop paper calendar into the company's shared electronic scheduler.

For the past year, a well-meaning colleague has devoted fifteen minutes of her break time each day to posting Jerry's schedule in the system and printing out notices of meetings and appointments he has been assigned to attend.

Verbal Notification

I've asked you to meet with me to discuss our concern that you are not making use of our computer-based tools, including the company's shared electronic scheduler. You also make only minimal use of the e-mail system to communicate with other departments and with clients.

Is there any reason I should know about that prevents you from using the computer tools?

We have in the past offered general classes for all employees on use of the computer, and I know you have attended them. I would like to ask the human resources department to establish a customized series of courses with a consultant.

MEMO TO FILE: Noting a request for action

Confidential: Personnel matter
Date: January 15, 20xx
Manager:
Regarding employee: Jerry Watson
Subject: Computer skills

I met today with Mr. Watson to discuss our concern that he is not making use of our computer-based tools, including the company's shared electronic scheduler. We also have determined that he is making only minimal use of the e-mail system to communicate with other departments and with clients.

I asked Mr. Watson if there was any reason I should know of that might prevent him from using the computer tools. He responded that he felt that he had no need for computers and could perform his job quite well using a typewriter.

We have in the past offered general classes for all employees on use of the computer and Mr. Watson has attended them, apparently without success. I have decided to ask the human resources department to establish a customized series of courses with a consultant. Mr. Watson agreed to take the courses.

MEMO TO FILE: Offer of assistance

Confidential: Personnel matter
Date: January 18, 20xx
Manager:
Regarding employee: Jerry Watson
Subject: Computer skills

The human resources department has set up a four-week series of courses on basic computer skills, tailored specially for Mr. Watson. The course will be given in two-hour blocks on Monday, Wednesday, and Friday and will begin on February 1.

Our goal is to help a valued employee update his skills so that he can make use of the organizational intranet as well as e-mail for contact with clients. Mr. Watson has promised to give his best efforts to the courses.

We will review progress on this matter on March 15.

PERFORMANCE EVALUATION: Acknowledging progress

Confidential: Personnel matter
Date: March 15, 20xx
Manager:
Regarding employee: Jerry Watson
Subject: Computer skills

According to the human resources department and his supervisors, Mr. Watson has demonstrated significant progress in using computer-based tools, including the integrated calendar and scheduling application, our corporate intranet, and e-mail services for clients and within the office.

Mr. Watson completed a four-week series of courses developed by human resources. At this time, the department recommends we consider a one-day refresher course in a month's time to deal with any remaining difficulties.

PERFORMANCE EVALUATION: Fails to meet expectations

Confidential: Personnel matter
Date: March 15, 20xx
Manager:
Regarding employee: Jerry Watson
Subject: Computer skills

According to the human resources department and his supervisors, Mr. Watson has failed to demonstrate significant progress in using the company's computer-based tools, including the integrated calendar and scheduling application, our corporate intranet, and e-mail services for clients and within the office.

Mr. Watson was offered a four-week series of courses developed by human resources. According to the trainers and his supervisors, though, he has not shown full commitment to use of the computer. At this time, the department does not recommend further expenditures of time or money without an indication by Mr. Watson that he is willing and able to devote sufficient effort to learning to use the computer tools.

At this time, we have decided to seek such a commitment from Mr. Watson before further training is considered. I will schedule a meeting including Mr. Watson and his direct supervisors for March 20. After a review of that meeting, we will decide whether to proceed with further training. We may also decide to transfer Mr. Watson to another appropriate job, if available, or to seek his termination from employment.

WRITTEN WARNING

Confidential: Personnel matter
Date: April 1, 20xx
Manager:
Regarding employee: Jerry Watson
Subject: Computer skills

According to the human resources department and your direct supervisors, you have not demonstrated significant progress in using computer-based tools, including the integrated calendar and scheduling application, our corporate intranet, and e-mail services for clients and within the office.

In January, you were offered a four-week series of courses developed by human resources. According to the trainers and your supervisors, though, you have not shown full commitment to use of the computer. At this time, the department does not recommend further expenditures of time or money without an indication by you that you are willing and able to devote sufficient effort to learning to use the computer tools.

At this time, we have decided to seek such a commitment before further training is considered. I will schedule a meeting with you and your direct supervisors for March 20. After a review of that meeting, your managers will decide whether to proceed with further training. We may also decide to transfer you to another appropriate job if available or to seek your termination from employment.

Safety Comes Last

State and federal inspectors come calling regularly, and the insurance company's inspectors make their own visits from time to time. They're checking up to see that occupational safety and health regulations are posted and that employees follow them.

The first target of the visitors is the organization itself. Laws, regulations, and components of workers compensation and other insurance policies require that a safe workplace be established and that employees are properly trained and supervised. The level of involvement ranges from detailed inspection of tools and machinery on a factory floor to safety shoes and fluorescent vests worn by construction and maintenance workers to installation of ergonomically designed chairs and office furniture for clerical staff.

The organization, then, has a responsibility to require that its employees follow regulations. It's not just corporate paternalism—organizations can be slapped with economic penalties from insurers and fines from government entities, and can open themselves to greater exposure in lawsuits.

It's no surprise, then, that companies require workers to be trained on job safety and can discipline or dismiss employees who violate the rules.

Which brings us to the case of Gilbert Arthur, a long-time and well-respected veteran of the shipping department. Mr. Arthur has a near-perfect attendance record, has always received positive evaluations from his supervisors, and knows the ins and outs of the organization about as well as anyone. He is also exceedingly stubborn.

Although the company has received satisfactory certification from state and federal agencies and its insurance carriers for its purchase and installation of improved material-handling, boxing, and crating equipment, the supervisor of the shipping department knows that he has a serious problem with one staffer, Mr. Arthur. He does not follow most of the required or recommended safety rules. The supervisor spends his days with an eye on the hallway so that he can spot an inspector—and send Mr. Arthur on a break.

Verbal Notification

I have asked you to meet with me to discuss a concern we have about your observance of safety rules in the workplace. As you know, we take such matters very seriously in accordance with federal and state laws as well as requirements from our insurance carriers.

We value you as an employee and wish you success in your career. However, we cannot permit continued disregard of OSHA and other safety rules.

I am going to ask that you attend a meeting this afternoon with a representative of the human resources department and your supervisor. They will devise a refresher course on the use of safety equipment and required practices. We expect the course will require about three days and will take place within the next week.

I will ask you to meet with me again in ten days to review your progress in this area, and we will conduct a formal employee evaluation with a focus on this issue in one month's time.

MEMO TO FILE: Noting a request for action

Confidential: Personnel matter
Date: January 15, 20xx
Manager:
Regarding employee: Gilbert Arthur
Subject: Safety regulations

I met today with Mr. Arthur to discuss a concern we have about his observance of safety rules in the workplace. I reminded him that we take such matters very seriously in accordance with federal and state laws as well as requirements from our insurance carriers.

I assured Mr. Arthur that we value him as an employee and wish him success in his career. However, I emphasized that we cannot permit continued disregard of OSHA and other safety rules.

I directed Mr. Arthur to attend a meeting this afternoon with a representative of the human resources department and his supervisor. I have arranged for them to devise a refresher course on the use of safety equipment and required practices. We expect the course will require about three days and will take place within the next week.

I asked Mr. Arthur to meet with me again in ten days to review his progress in this area. We will also conduct a formal employee evaluation with a focus on this issue in one month's time.

MEMO TO FILE: Offer of assistance

Confidential: Personnel matter
Date: January 18, 20xx
Manager:
Regarding employee: Gilbert Arthur
Subject: Safety regulations

Mr. Arthur has agreed to take a three-day refresher course on the use of safety equipment and practices, as developed by the human resources department in cooperation with his departmental supervisors.

I have directed Mr. Arthur to meet with me again in ten days to review his progress in this area. We will also conduct a formal employee evaluation with a focus on this issue in one month's time.

PERFORMANCE EVALUATION: Acknowledging progress

Confidential: Personnel matter
Date: March 1, 20xx
Manager:
Regarding employee: Gilbert Arthur
Subject: Safety regulations

I am informed by departmental supervisors and the human resources department that Mr. Arthur has demonstrated significant improvement in adherence to rules on use of safety equipment and safety procedures.

Mr. Arthur participated in a specialized training session designed and implemented by the human resources department, and according to his supervisors he cooperated fully. We will continue to monitor his progress in this area, including another performance evaluation on April 1.

PERFORMANCE EVALUATION: Fails to meet expectations

Confidential: Personnel matter
Date: March 1, 20xx
Manager:
Regarding employee: Gilbert Arthur
Subject: Safety regulations

I am informed by departmental supervisors and the human resources department that Mr. Arthur has failed to demonstrate significant improvement in adherence to organizational rules on use of safety equipment and proper safety procedures.

Mr. Arthur participated in a specialized training session designed and implemented by the human resources department, produced in response to a finding on January 15 that he was not following regulations as required for his position.

With this evaluation, we are putting Mr. Arthur on notice that we expect full cooperation on all matters of safety equipment and procedures immediately. We will meet again on March 15 and review the situation. If there is not a marked improvement in his commitment to safety in the workplace at that time, we will decide whether to proceed with further training. We may also decide to transfer Mr. Arthur to another appropriate job, if available, or to seek his termination from employment.

WRITTEN WARNING

Confidential: Personnel matter
Date: March 1, 20xx
Manager:
Regarding employee: Gilbert Arthur
Subject: Safety regulations

I am informed by departmental supervisors and the human resources department that you have failed to demonstrate significant improvement in adherence to organizational rules on use of safety equipment and proper safety procedures.

You participated in a specialized training session designed and implemented by the human resources department, produced in response to a finding on January 15 that you were not following regulations as required for this position.

With this memo, we are putting you on notice that we expect full cooperation on all matters of safety equipment and procedures immediately. We will meet again on March 15 and review the situation. If there is not a marked improvement in your commitment to safety in the workplace at that time, we will decide whether to proceed with further training. We may also decide to transfer you to another appropriate job, if available, or to seek your termination from employment.

Chapter 5

INFORMATION AND SECURITY

YOU CAN LOCK the doors and windows, place padlocks on the file cabinets, and paper the walls with reminders, warnings, and threats. But in this modern age, none of these steps will come close to safeguarding the true value of an organization.

At the dawn of the industrial age, a company's success was often tied to its physical inventions—a better way to run a mill or a press or a planting machine. The equipment could be locked up, new ideas could be patented, and organizational records could be kept under lock and key. At the same time, a manager could directly supervise and account for the productivity of the workers. It was literally a matter of counting beans, plows, or yards of fabric produced.

Today we are deep into the information age. An organization's most valuable asset is knowledge: how to perform a service or produce a product of high quality and low cost; exacting details of the preferences and requirements of every customer or client; automated procedures to monitor and manage; quality control, inventory, manufacturing, shipping, billing, and minute-by-minute appraisals of financial conditions.

Some of the most successful modern companies don't even have a physical product in the old sense. Think of eBay, PayPal, and Google. Their business is based on intellectual property that resides in the minds of their employees and the memories of the hard disks of their computers. The entire business process of these companies can exist without the need for paper, pen, file folder, rubber stamp, carbon paper, paper clip . . . you get the idea. Their business is an idea, put into motion.

This is all wondrous stuff and by no means limited to the young stars of the Web. Here in Massachusetts, where the authors of this book live and work, our incomes arrive in the form of an electronic deposit in an online checking account. We pay our bills without touching a paper check, and reconcile the "books" with the click of a mouse. The results are sent by e-mail to a dedicated accountant who lives 250 miles away and with whom we have not met in several years. Monthly payments to the tax department are made through a Web page.

Then there is this book. In your hands you hold a physical document, printed with ink on paper. For almost all of its existence before the presses began to roll, though, the manuscript existed as an idea and a draft that was stored as magnetic bits in one or another computer.

What would happen if someone were to do any of these things:

- Steal an idea?
- Walk away with a secret?
- Release the hard-earned contents of our electronic Rolodex?
- Accidentally or maliciously destroy information that is at the heart of our business?

Any organization that has hopes of surviving has to have this sort of high-tech paranoia as part of its operational plan.

Here's the rule: What happens in the place where you earn your wages stays there unless it is in your job description to go out and sell a service or product or otherwise represent the organization. Many employers dealing with intellectual property as a core asset will require staffers to sign nondisclosure agreements or other contracts that are intended to protect the organization by the threat of a lawsuit. Other companies may make it an element of the employee manual that unauthorized disclosure of information is cause for discipline or dismissal.

Unless you're working at the CIA or a military base, chances are your handbag, briefcase, or pockets are not going to be searched each time you enter or leave the workplace. But a huge amount of data can easily be hidden on a tiny memory "key" about the size of a stick of gum.

Even more frightening to many companies is the prospect of employees opening the doors to the company's intellectual treasures by sending information by e-mail or by the accidental or intentional release of logins and passwords to computer systems.

Ya Got Trouble

Mary Tobak is not a double agent. She has no intention of compromising the efforts of the organization by releasing its secrets to competitors, clients, or the merely curious.

She also had no concept of the danger she was creating when she brought home a tiny slip of paper with her user ID and password written on it. She thought it might be interesting to show her young nephew, a bright high school kid, some of the fancy new software tools that had recently been added to her job equipment. She had no idea he would share the password with his buddies and one of them would post information in his blog.

Verbal Notification

I've asked you to meet with me to discuss a concern we have about a possible violation of our procedures for computer security. It appears that your user ID and password have been disclosed to someone outside of the organization, and we have experienced several attempts to enter into our system from unauthorized locations.

Do you have any idea how your computer ID and password were exposed in this way?

We have taken measures to block access to our computers through your prior account. Before you resume use of the organization's management information system, I want you to meet with a representative of the computer department and the human resources department this afternoon to review security and proper usage policies.

MEMO TO FILE: Noting a request for action

Confidential: Personnel matter
Date: January 15, 20xx
Manager:
Regarding employee: Mary Tobak
Subject: Improper computer security practices

I met today with Ms. Tobak to discuss a concern we have about a possible violation of our procedures for computer security. I explained to her that it appears her user ID and password have been disclosed to someone outside of the organization, and we have experienced several attempts to enter our system from unauthorized locations.

I asked her how this might have occurred. She told me she had signed on to the system from home to show a young nephew some of the advanced computer systems she was working with, and she said it was possible that he might have made note of her user ID and password. She apologized for causing a problem and promised not to make such an unauthorized use of the system again.

I told her that we consider such an action to be a potentially serious breach of organizational security. We have taken measures to block access to our computers through Ms. Tobak's prior account. I instructed her to meet with a representative of the computer department and the human resources department this afternoon to review security and proper usage policies.

I have asked the computer department to report back to me by the end of the day about the results of the meeting with Ms. Tobak and to inform me whether they feel any further action is required. They will also maintain a daily log of all access to the computer and all sites visited by Ms. Tobak and anyone else who might be using her user ID.

Further, I have informed Ms. Tobak that we will review this situation again in ten days and once more on the occasion of her next scheduled employee evaluation, on March 1.

MEMO TO FILE: Offer of assistance

Confidential: Personnel matter
Date: January 18, 20xx
Manager:
Regarding employee: Mary Tobak
Subject: Improper computer security practices

The computer department has recommended that before Ms. Tobak be allowed to resume use of system resources, she be given a refresher course on security policies and that she also be given a more limited level of access to sensitive data as appropriate to her job description.

I agree with these recommendations and will inform Ms. Tobak of them tomorrow morning. I have directed the human resources department to develop the refresher course on computer security together with the computer department and to begin training within the next week.

We will review this situation again in ten days and once more on the occasion of her next scheduled employee evaluation, on March 1.

PERFORMANCE EVALUATION: Acknowledging progress

Confidential: Personnel matter
Date: March 1, 20xx
Manager:
Regarding employee: Mary Tobak
Subject: Improper computer security practices

Ms. Tobak has demonstrated significant improvement in her understanding of and compliance with computer security.

She successfully completed a two-day refresher course on computer security. According to the computer department, there have been no further instances of actual or attempted improper access to organizational resources related to Ms. Tobak's user ID.

PERFORMANCE EVALUATION: Fails to meet expectations

Confidential: Personnel matter
Date: March 1, 20xx
Manager:
Regarding employee: Mary Tobak
Subject: Improper computer security practices

According to the computer department, there have been further ongoing attempts to access organizational resources using both the original and revised user ID and password of Ms. Tobak. Since the original account was blocked, the computer department considers the recent attempts to enter the system from unauthorized locations to be a new breach of security.

Ms. Tobak was directed to take a refresher course on computer security after an initial concern was noted in January. At the same time, the computer department instituted a daily log of all use of her account.

Based on this information, it is apparent that Ms. Tobak has failed to meet our expectations regarding computer security. Her access to the computer has been suspended effective today, and I will meet with her supervisors and representatives of the computer department on March 2. At that meeting we will decide whether to reassign Ms. Tobak to an appropriate position, if one is available, seek further remedial training, or terminate her employment.

WRITTEN WARNING

Confidential: Personnel matter
Date: March 1, 20xx
Manager:
Regarding employee: Mary Tobak
Subject: Improper computer security practices

According to the computer department, there have been further ongoing attempts to access organizational resources using both your original and revised user ID and password. Since the original account was blocked after an earlier incident in January, the computer department considers the recent attempts to enter the system from unauthorized locations to be a new breach of security.

You were directed to take a refresher course on computer security after an initial concern was noted in January. At the same time, the computer department instituted a daily log of all use of your account.

Based on this information, it is apparent that you have failed to meet our expectations regarding computer security. Your access to the computer has been suspended effective today, and I will meet with your supervisors and representatives of the computer department on March 2. At that meeting we will decide whether to reassign you to an appropriate position, if one is available, seek further remedial training, or terminate your employment.

Lost in Translation

One of the perks of being a sales representative these days is the issuance of a fancy laptop computer that can communicate over the Internet to display a full database of product and service descriptions and pricing. In many organizations, the laptop also includes proprietary tools for design or configuration of custom products or services.

Every employee issued a laptop is given training on how to use it and instructions on how to guard against the theft, loss, or misuse of this valuable asset.

Mark Barsani is a very capable sales representative, known for going the extra mile to make his clients happy . . . and to meet his quotas. On his most recent sales trip, though, his laptop went missing on Monday in Minneapolis, but the loss wasn't reported to the information technology department until his return on Friday afternoon.

Verbal Notification

I've asked you to meet with me to discuss your recent loss of a company laptop. Although we ask that all employees take every precaution to avoid loss or theft of company property, especially laptop computers that could be used to access proprietary information, we do realize that not all incidents can be avoided.

As I understand it, you informed the information technology department on Friday that your laptop was stolen from your rental car on Monday.

Our company policy, as outlined in the employee manual and in the training sessions given with the issuance of a laptop, requires any loss of a laptop to be reported immediately. A representative of the information technology department is on call seven days a week at all times for this purpose. Upon notification, we immediately shut down existing user IDs to prevent unauthorized access, and we conduct an audit of the known contents of the laptop to assess whether further action is required.

Can you tell me why you waited four days to notify us of the loss of the laptop?

MEMO TO FILE: Noting a request for action

Confidential: Personnel matter
Date: January 15, 20xx
Manager:
Regarding employee: Mark Barsani
Subject: Computer security

I met today with Mr. Barsani to discuss his recent loss of a company laptop while on a business trip. As I understand it, he informed the information technology department on Friday that his laptop was stolen from his rental car the previous Monday.

I reviewed with Mr. Barsani that although we ask that all employees take every precaution to avoid loss or theft of company property, and especially laptop computers that could be used to access proprietary information, we do realize that not all incidents can be avoided.

However, our company policy, as outlined in the employee manual and in the training sessions given with the issuance of a laptop, directs that any loss of a laptop must be reported immediately. A representative of the information technology department is on call seven days a week at all times for this purpose. Upon notification, we immediately shut down existing user IDs to prevent unauthorized access, and we conduct an audit of the known contents of the laptop to assess whether further action is required.

Mr. Barsani told me that he notified local police about the loss of the laptop and hoped it might be found before he left the area.

I have directed Mr. Barsani to meet with a representative of the information technology department and the human resources department today to review our policies on use of company laptops and our policies on computer security. I will await a report from those two departments before deciding whether further action is required.

MEMO TO FILE: Offer of assistance

Confidential: Personnel matter
Date: January 18, 20xx
Manager:
Regarding employee: Mark Barsani
Subject: Computer security

The information technology department has recommended that Mr. Barsani be given a refresher course on company policy for the use of laptop computers before he is issued a new machine. I agree with that recommendation and with this memo I direct Mr. Barsani to contact the department to arrange for the course immediately.

Further, the information technology department has recommended that Mr. Barsani be given a PDA instead of a laptop. Using a personal data assistant device will allow Mr. Barsani to sign on to the organization computer system to send and receive e-mail and to check inventory and other reports, but the PDA does not hold data in storage. This is appropriate for his job description and reduces the risk to the company. Our newest systems include a fingerprint recognition module that prevents unauthorized access even if the password and user ID are compromised. I have also agreed with that recommendation.

I have directed Mr. Barsani to meet with a representative of the information technology department within the next week to receive the new PDA and undergo training in its use.

PERFORMANCE EVALUATION: Acknowledging progress

Confidential: Personnel matter
Date: March 1, 20xx
Manager:
Regarding employee: Mark Barsani
Subject: Computer security

Since January, Mr. Barsani has demonstrated commitment to maintaining the security of computer information. He received a new PDA that is appropriate for his job description and has followed the directions of the information technology department concerning its proper use.

PERFORMANCE EVALUATION: Fails to meet expectations

Confidential: Personnel matter
Date: April 1, 20xx
Manager:
Regarding employee: Mark Barsani
Subject: Computer security

For the second time in two months, Mr. Barsani has acted in a way that could have compromised the integrity of the organization's information technology files. I am informed that logs maintained by the computer department show that he has been using his PDA for personal Internet use. Doing so could result in a hacker attempting an unauthorized access to our system.

Mr. Barsani has failed to demonstrate proper understanding and adherence to company policy in this area.

With this evaluation, I am directing Mr. Barsani to meet with me tomorrow morning at 9 A.M. We will discuss the situation, and then I will meet with his departmental supervisors.

Within the next five days, we will decide whether to reassign Mr. Barsani to an appropriate position, if one is available, seek further remedial training, or terminate his employment.

WRITTEN WARNING

Confidential: Personnel matter
Date: April 1, 20xx
Manager:
Regarding employee: Mark Barsani
Subject: Computer security

I would like you to meet with me tomorrow morning at 9 A.M. to discuss our belief that you have failed to demonstrate proper understanding and adherence to company policy in regard to computer security.

For the second time in two months, you have acted in a way that could have compromised the integrity of the organization's information technology files. I am informed that logs maintained by the computer department show that you have been using your PDA for personal Internet use. Doing so could result in a hacker attempting an unauthorized access to our system.

We will discuss the situation, and then I will meet with your departmental supervisors.

Within the next five days, we will decide whether to reassign you to an appropriate position, if one is available, seek further remedial training, or terminate your employment.

A Little Business on the Side

Jimmy Eastham is usually at his desk fifteen or twenty minutes before his scheduled starting time and is rarely the first one out the door. His work as a customer service representative is well regarded by both his clients and his supervisors, and he has an unbroken string of positive performance evaluations in his personnel file.

As far as his manager and those around him could tell, Jimmy always devoted his full attention to his job. But a new software program installed by the information technology department that monitors the Internet usage of all employees tells a different story. It shows that in addition to his official duties, Jimmy has also been maintaining a very busy (and apparently lucrative) sideline buying and selling collectible baseball cards through an online auction site.

The analysis shows Jimmy has figured out how to get around the organization's official internal Web page and gain access to the outside world. The computer technician who discovered the situation noted that although there was no evidence that problematic consequences had occurred, the workaround had exposed the organization's proprietary computer system to hacking or infiltration of viruses from the outside.

Verbal Notification

I've asked you to meet with me to discuss information we have received that you are making extensive use of company computer resources for personal purposes. As the employee manual states, all communication using corporate intranet, Internet, and e-mail is subject to monitoring by the information resources department. As part of ordinary logging of activity, that department has reported that in the past month you have spent as much as 25 percent of your time at work visiting Web sites that are unrelated to your job description.

In addition to what appears to be a misuse of company resources, the information resources department reports that you are using methods to get around blocks put in place by computer managers to prevent access to non-business-related Web sites. Use of such "proxy" or "anonymous surfing" tools are specifically prohibited in the employee manual.

Is there any explanation for this?

MEMO TO FILE: Noting a request for action

Confidential: Personnel matter
Date: January 15, 20xx
Manager:
Regarding employee: Jimmy Eastham
Subject: Personal use of corporate computer resources

I met today with Mr. Eastham to discuss information we have received that he has been making extensive use of company computer resources for personal purposes. As part of ordinary logging of activity, the information resources department has reported that in the past month he has spent as much as 25 percent of his time at work visiting Web sites that are unrelated to his job description.

The log includes extended periods of time logged on to eBay and other auction sites. Our own investigation has determined that Mr. Eastham buys and sells baseball cards through an online Web site.

As the employee manual states, all communication using corporate intranet, Internet, and e-mail is subject to monitoring by the information resources department. Further, the computer department has put into place safeguards that block access to many known Web sites unrelated to our core business. These include auction sites, online shopping, personal banking, and inappropriate sites including those devoted to politics, religion, and sexual content.

The information resources department reports that Mr. Eastham has been using methods to get around blocks put in place by computer managers to prevent access to non-business-related Web sites. Use of such "proxy" or "anonymous surfing" tools are specifically prohibited in the employee manual.

When I asked Mr. Eastham about these activities, he at first denied they were occurring. He then said that he was only accessing a few sites during his lunch hour. When I told him we had logs indicating much more extensive use of the Internet than that, and that we had determined he had been using a workaround to get through barriers put in place by the computer department, he declined to discuss the matter further.

I told him that effective immediately he was not to use the computer for any purposes other than those directly related to his job description, and I emphasized that the information resources department would be reviewing the logs of his Internet usage daily and sharing that information with his department head.

I told Mr. Eastham that I wanted him to meet with his supervisor and a representative of the information resources department tomorrow morning to discuss company rules regarding use of the Internet for personal uses, and that I would schedule a special performance evaluation on this issue for February 1.

MEMO TO FILE: Offer of assistance

Confidential: Personnel matter
Date: January 18, 20xx
Manager:
Regarding employee: Jimmy Eastham
Subject: Personal use of corporate computer resources

According to his supervisors, and in keeping with his job description, Mr. Eastham does require regular use of the Internet. However, the information resources department has recommended that Mr. Eastham be given a limited account that will be actively monitored by their staff.

Further, the computer department has asked that a representative of their department and the human resources department meet with Mr. Eastham within the next forty-eight hours to review the employee manual as it applies to this area.

I have approved both recommendations. We will review this matter in a special performance evaluation on February 1.

PERFORMANCE EVALUATION: Acknowledging progress

Confidential: Personnel matter
Date: February 1, 20xx
Manager:
Regarding employee: Jimmy Eastham
Subject: Personal use of corporate computer resources

According to his supervisors, and based on monitoring by the information resources department, it is evident that Mr. Eastham has ended his use of corporate computer resources for personal purposes and has not attempted to circumvent safeguards through the use of proxies or redirection of traffic.

We will continue to electronically monitor his account until further notice.

PERFORMANCE EVALUATION: Fails to meet expectations

Confidential: Personnel matter
Date: February 1, 20xx
Manager:
Regarding employee: Jimmy Eastham
Subject: Personal use of corporate computer resources

According to his supervisors, and based on monitoring by the information resources department, it is evident that Mr. Eastham has failed to meet our expectations and is continuing to use corporate computer resources for personal purposes. This was noted in electronic monitoring of e-mail and Internet traffic from his workstation and logs that show he continues to circumvent safeguards through the use of proxies or redirection of traffic.

Because of the specific warnings given to Mr. Eastham on January 15 and January 18, we have decided to seek his immediate termination from employment. I will forward his file to the human resources department today and ask that they meet with him immediately and dismiss him from employment.

WRITTEN WARNING

Confidential: Personnel matter
Date: February 1, 20xx
Manager:
Regarding employee: Jimmy Eastham
Subject: Personal use of corporate computer resources

We have determined that you have failed to meet our expectations and in recent weeks have continued to use corporate computer resources for personal purposes.

With this memo, I am directing you to meet with the head of the human resources department today at 4 P.M.

Chapter 6

HARASSMENT

AT ITS BASE, harassment is words or actions—based on race, sex, religion, national origin, age, or disability—that create a hostile work environment or establish an improper quid pro quo.

Let's define the three most important of those terms:

- Harassment includes demeaning actions and words and implied or explicit threats of violence.
- A hostile work environment is a place of employment that a complainant reasonably finds to be inherently intimidating, hostile, or abusive. For its part, the employer can make reasonable judgments about the severity of alleged harassment, its frequency, and whether it interferes with the complainant's ability to perform his or her job.
- Quid pro quo harassment involves unwelcome sexual advances or other verbal or physical conduct that is intended to extract compliance in return for a reward including job advancement, job retention, or other employment-related issues.

To get down to specifics, here are some examples of harassment:

- Implying, or demanding, that a subordinate provide sexual favors in order to keep a job, gain a promotion, or be able to perform a job
- Making highly personal and unwelcome comments about a coworker's clothing or physical appearance
- Inappropriate or unwelcome physical contact
- Discussing sex or telling sexually explicit jokes in an inappropriate situation
- Using office electronic networks and e-mails to transmit sexually explicit images or text in an inappropriate situation

Preventing Harassment

Make sure your company or organization has a clear and precise policy that prohibits harassment of any type, in accordance with federal, state, and local law. The policy should instruct employees on how to report harassment and specify the steps that the organization will take in response.

Many employers require staff to attend training sessions intended to prevent harassment and discrimination and remind employees of the processes in place to allow pursuit of complaints. Similar sessions are conducted for managers.

Dealing with a Harassment Complaint

If you receive a complaint of discrimination or harassment (or if you discern a possible violation of rights yourself) the most important thing you can do is this: Treat the situation seriously and carefully.

The worst things you can do are these:

- Ignore a complaint.
- Fail to follow established policies in your company or organization.
- Belittle a complaint.
- Demean the complainant.
- Retaliate against the complainant.

This applies whether the complaint proves to be legitimate or not. Assume that every complaint is legitimate, and conduct a proper investigation. Failure to properly handle an allegation of discrimination or harassment can lead to a lawsuit related to the process itself or to punitive damages in a legal finding or settlement.

On the plus side, a professional and compassionate response to a complaint can contribute to a better workplace for all employees. An employee who feels that his or her complaint is given proper attention may be less likely to raise the stakes by involving a government agency or an attorney.

Although it is improper to retaliate against a complainant, it is not illegal to apply disciplinary procedures against an employee who is determined to have made malicious or demonstrably untrue or unfair allegations in the workplace. This is an area where the involvement of legal counsel would be very valuable.

The Proper Path
Your company or organization should have a published policy that commits to a workplace free of dis-

crimination and harassment and that specifies the steps for employees and supervisors to follow if a violation is alleged. If you have any doubts about what should be included in that policy, consult a human resources expert or an attorney.

The next step is to follow those steps. Do not make an exception for someone you believe to be more worthy or less worthy in making a complaint.

Keep careful notes on any interviews you conduct, including dates and times. Gather any documents related to the claim, including e-mails.

Do not destroy any evidence, including electronic files and e-mails. Anything you do to remove evidence has the appearance of covering up guilt.

Notify anyone in the company or organization who needs to know about the proceedings; this chain of command should be spelled out in the published policy. In most situations the list should include supervisors, your human resources department, and the in-house or outside legal counsel.

If the allegations involve you or your direct supervisor, make certain that full notice of the complaint is given to legal counsel and top management. Do not attempt to do the two irreconcilable tasks of defending yourself at the same time as attempting to impartially represent the company or institution.

At the same time do not discuss the situation with anyone who is not involved in the claim. Assume that everything you say will be repeated to one side or the other—the accused or the accuser—and that your words could end being part of legal proceedings related to the complaint. Even worse, you could end up being a party in a personal defamation lawsuit.

Some companies or institutions have a policy that takes control of the investigation and disposal of any complaint out of the supervisor's hands and places it with an outside professional.

Once the investigation is completed, take reasonable and appropriate action. Depending on the nature of the complaint and any evidence you have gathered—and in keeping with your company or organization's published policies—discipline can range from a warning or a negative employee evaluation to a suspension, demotion, or termination.

The final step is to document your actions and provide notification of your findings and steps taken to the complainant.

Way Too Friendly

Harry Johnson is a back-slapper. He's also a neck-rubber, a shoulder-massager, and an occasional friendly hugger.

To hear Harry tell it, he's just a friendly guy. Many of the staffers he supervises don't mind his physical attention. Hard at work, hunched over their keyboards, they're happy to receive a bit of a break from the boss.

But some of the people in his department don't appreciate being touched in the workplace. To some it's annoying, and to others it approaches or even crosses the line into sexual harassment. Now it has reached the level where an employee has notified the human resources department. There hasn't yet been a formal complaint, but if the situation is not addressed, there will be. There is the possibility of a lawsuit.

A WORD *to the* WISE

At the first indication of a possible problem, immediately get your human resources department or in-house or outside counsel involved. You can listen to any reports made by complainants or by a person accused of improper conduct, but you should not make any responses that might be interpreted as condoning or dismissing possible misconduct. You should also not make any promises to complainants or an accused employee other than a commitment to investigate the situation. Some organizations direct any supervisor who is notified of a possible problem in this area to stay out of any discussions and instead leave the issue to be handled by the human resources or legal department.

Verbal Notification

I've asked you to meet with me to discuss a matter of personal conduct. First of all, I want to assure you that we respect and appreciate your work for the company.

It has been brought to my attention that some of the staff members you supervise say they are uncomfortable with what they describe as physical touching by you. This has not risen to the level of a formal complaint, and we hope it will not become one.

However, I must emphasize to you that this organization has a zero-tolerance policy regarding physical or sexual harassment. Although you may consider touching another person to be a friendly or innocuous gesture, this kind of contact might be interpreted by others as inappropriate, discomforting, or threatening.

I am directing you to immediately stop any such physical contact with coworkers and especially those members of staff under your supervision.

I have set up an appointment for 1 P.M. today with a representative of the human resources department to discuss the matter and to schedule any training or advisement they recommend.

Again, I want to reiterate that we hope that this issue does not require any further action, but it is important that you understand that we take such situations very seriously. This is an essential element of our employee manual and a matter of law.

I will be monitoring this situation through reports from the human resources department as well as your department head.

MEMO TO FILE: Noting a request for action

Confidential: Personnel matter
Date: January 15, 20xx
Manager:
Regarding employee: Harry Johnson
Subject: Personal conduct

I met today with Mr. Johnson to discuss a matter of personal conduct. It has been brought to my attention that some of the members of staff he supervises say they are uncomfortable with what they describe as physical touching. As of this date, this has not risen to the level of a formal complaint.

I assured Mr. Johnson we respect and appreciate his work for the company. However, I emphasized to him that this organization has a zero-tolerance policy regarding physical or sexual harassment. I told him that although he may consider touching another person to be a friendly or innocuous gesture, this kind of contact might be interpreted by others as inappropriate, discomforting, or threatening.

I directed him to immediately stop any such physical contact with coworkers and especially those members of staff under his supervision.

I set up an appointment for 1 P.M. today with a representative of the human resources department to discuss the matter and to schedule any training or advisement they recommend.

I reiterated to Mr. Johnson that we hope that this issue does not require any further action, but it is important that he understand that we take such situations very seriously. This is an essential element of our employee manual and a matter of law.

I will be monitoring this situation through reports from the human resources department as well as his department head.

MEMO TO FILE: Offer of assistance

Confidential: Personnel matter
Date: January 18, 20xx
Manager:
Regarding employee: Harry Johnson
Subject: Personal conduct

I today received a report from the director of the human resources department in regard to the personal conduct of Harry Johnson. (See file dated January 15, 20xx, about this situation.)

The human resources department has determined that Mr. Johnson should undergo a three-day training course about sexual harassment prevention. This is an intensive version of the basic class that is given to all employees and supervisors at the time of hiring and repeated at least once every eighteen months.

Because of the sensitive nature of this issue, I have asked the director of human resources to brief me personally on progress at the end of the training session and weekly thereafter for a period of at least eight weeks. I have asked him to advise me if there is any further action that needs to be taken by this department.

PERFORMANCE EVALUATION: Acknowledging progress

Confidential: Personnel matter
Date: April 1, 20xx
Manager:
Regarding employee: Harry Johnson
Subject: Personal conduct

I today received an update from the director of the human resources department in regard to the personal conduct of Harry Johnson. (See files dated January 15, 20xx, and January 18, 20xx, about this situation.)

According to the human resources department, there has been no reported recurrence of the concerns first registered in January. In addition, no formal action has been brought by any employee in the period.

Mr. Johnson completed a three-day training course about sexual harassment prevention in January. At the time I asked the director of human resources to brief me personally on progress at the end of the training session and weekly thereafter for a period of at least eight weeks.

I wish to thank Mr. Johnson for his cooperation in the training session and his apparent efforts in the subsequent time period.

PERFORMANCE EVALUATION: Fails to meet expectations

Confidential: Personnel matter
Date: April 1, 20xx
Manager:
Regarding employee: Harry Johnson
Subject: Personal conduct

I today received an update from the director of the human resources department in regard to the personal conduct of Harry Johnson. (See files dated January 15, 20xx, and January 18, 20xx, about this situation.)

According to the human resources department, there were two new reports of physical contact between Mr. Johnson and two female workers under his supervision. Although the workers have filed no formal complaint, this may represent a serious violation of the employee code of conduct.

With this memo, I am requesting the director of the human resources department and our in-house counsel to investigate the situation. Because of the sensitive nature of this matter, these two members of senior management will decide whether there are any grounds for further action, which could include discipline, reassignment to a nonmanagement position, or termination from employment.

WRITTEN WARNING

Confidential: Personnel matter
Date: April 1, 20xx
Manager:
Regarding employee: Harry Johnson
Subject: Personal conduct

I today received an update from the director of the human resources department regarding your personal conduct as a manager. This is in regard to previous informal complaints of physical contact brought to our attention in January of this year by several members of your department.

According to the human resources department, there have been two new complaints of physical contact between you and two workers under your supervision. Although the workers have filed no formal complaint, this may represent a serious violation of the employee code of conduct.

I am requesting the director of the human resources department and our in-house counsel to investigate the situation. Because of the sensitive nature of this matter, these two members of senior management will decide whether there are any grounds for further action, which could include discipline, reassignment to a nonmanagement position, or termination from employment.

Romance in the Workplace

In a perfect world, this would never happen: A supervisor becomes romantically involved with a subordinate. Regardless of who initiates the relationship, this is a landmine waiting to be triggered. If the romance continues, there may be concerns about a special relationship that is to the detriment of others. If the relationship ends, there is the possibility of loss of productivity in the department and even a chance of legal entanglements.

Some human resources and legal experts refer to this as a "dual relationship." One relationship takes place within the boundaries of the workplace, and the other is a personal relationship. If two people are able to keep the two relations completely separate—a very difficult task—there is no problem. If personal interests and concerns move into the workplace, there is a conflict of interest or possible disruption for the organization.

Katie Hertz is manager of the employee benefits department, with a staff of six reporting directly to her. Three months after the hiring of Donald Jones, she began dating him. Although they were very discreet in the workplace, in the small office, little can be kept completely secret.

In this case, we are dealing with a relationship freely entered into. Later in this chapter we'll consider a more sinister possibility. Here are some of the possible problems that could be engendered by romance in the workplace:

- Other staffers may perceive favoritism in assignments, pay, and access.
- Staffers may feel they were denied promotion, extra benefits, or plum assignments because of the special relationship in the office.
- If a relationship ends, the subordinate may claim he or she has been discriminated against in promotion, assignments, and compensation.
- The organization could find itself entangled in a sexual harassment or discrimination suit.

There are no federal or state laws that specifically make dating between employees illegal. However, some companies and other organizations may have a policy that prohibits such personal behavior or requires that management be notified and changes in supervision put into place.

The employee handbook should be very specific about organizational policy, and the issue should be discussed with new employees and reinforced with the existing workforce on a regular basis. The handbook should also advise managers on how to deal with situations that may arise due to dating between employees.

In most instances, there will be two sets of memos and employee evaluations—one for the supervisor and one for the staffer. In some organizations, an attorney may recommend that for privacy purposes, the name of the second party in each file be identified with a pseudonym or code. A separate document, held separate from the individual personnel files of the two individuals, may list actual names.

Verbal Notification

I've asked you to meet with me to discuss a matter of personal conduct that in our judgment has a potential impact on your ability to fulfill your responsibilities as a supervisor.

I want you to know that we value your commitment to the organization and your work very highly. We want to see you succeed and have every opportunity for further advancement. We also respect your right to privacy outside of the workplace.

It has come to our attention that you have established a personal relationship with someone you supervise. As you know, the employee manual requires that any supervisor make such a situation known to his or her department head; in most situations, this would require that someone else be assigned supervision.

Can you confirm that you have established a personal relationship with someone you supervise?

Your department head says you did not notify him of the relationship. Is that correct?

MEMO TO FILE: Noting a request for action

Confidential: Personnel matter
Date: January 15, 20xx
Manager:
Regarding employee: Katie Hertz
Subject: Personal conduct

I met today with Katie Hertz to discuss a matter of personal conduct that in our judgment has a potential impact on her ability to fulfill her responsibilities as a supervisor.

It has come to our attention Ms. Hertz has established a personal relationship with someone she supervises. The employee manual requires that any supervisor make such a situation known to his or her department head. We do this to avoid the possibility of favoritism or unfair treatment in the workplace. We are also committed to preventing sexual harassment in the workplace.

In this situation, our general policy calls for the reassignment of an employee to a different supervisor whenever possible. We may also change a job description including a transfer to a different department.

In our meeting today, Ms. Hertz confirmed that she has established a personal relationship with Mr. X, a junior employee in her department. She said that the relationship became "serious" only in the past ten days and that she had intended to meet with her department head this week to advise him of the situation. She apologized for the delay.

I told Ms. Hertz that we wanted her to know that we value her commitment to the organization and her work very highly. We want to see her succeed and have every opportunity for further advancement. We also respect her right to privacy outside of the workplace.

However, her delay in notifying her department head was a violation of the employee rules. I asked her to immediately schedule a meeting to discuss the situation and to follow all rules regarding personal relations between employees. I will seek an update from her department head within one business week.

MEMO TO FILE: Offer of assistance

Confidential: Personnel matter
Date: January 18, 20xx
Manager:
Regarding employee: Katie Hertz
Subject: Personal conduct

This is a follow-up on a meeting held with Katie Hertz on January 15 regarding a matter of personal conduct that in our judgment has a potential impact on her ability to fulfill her responsibilities as a supervisor.

It has come to our attention that Ms. Hertz has established a personal relationship with someone she supervises. The employee manual requires that any supervisor make such a situation known to his or her department head. We do this to avoid the possibility of favoritism or unfair treatment in the workplace. We are also committed to preventing sexual harassment in the workplace.

At the January 15 meeting, Ms. Hertz confirmed that she has established a personal relationship with Mr. X, a junior employee in her department. She said that the relationship had become "serious" only in the past ten days and that she had intended to meet with her department head this week to advise him of the situation. She apologized for the delay.

In this situation, our general policy calls for the reassignment of an employee to a different supervisor whenever possible. We may also change a job description, including a transfer to a different department.

I told Ms. Hertz that we wanted her to know that we value her commitment to the organization and her work very highly. We want to see her succeed and have every opportunity for further advancement. We also respect her right to privacy outside of the workplace.

I directed Ms. Hertz to immediately meet with her department head to discuss the situation and seek guidance.

I have subsequently heard from her department head that Ms. Hertz did come in for a meeting. A subsequent private meeting was held between the department head and Mr. X.

As a result of that session, Mr. X was offered a choice between a different position in another department or a change in supervisor from Ms. Hertz to another manager. I have asked that a formal report on a transfer of supervision or job responsibilities be appended to this file when it is available.

PERFORMANCE EVALUATION: Acknowledging progress

Confidential: Personnel matter
Date: April 1, 20xx
Manager:
Regarding employee: Katie Hertz
Subject: Personal conduct

I refer to a January 18, 20xx, memo to file about Ms. Hertz's personal relationship with a member of her staff. This situation has now been dealt with in accordance with the rules set forth in the employee manual. Ms. Hertz demonstrated full cooperation with the human resources department and her department head in working with them to change the supervision of Mr. X.

I have reiterated to Ms. Hertz that we value her commitment to the organization and her work very highly. We want to see her succeed and have every opportunity for further advancement. We also respect her right to privacy outside of the workplace. The only reason for our involvement in a personal matter such as this was to seek to avoid complications that can arise when there is a relationship between a supervisor and an employee that goes beyond the office setting.

PERFORMANCE EVALUATION: Fails to meet expectations

Confidential: Personnel matter
Date: April 1, 20xx
Manager:
Regarding employee: Katie Hertz
Subject: Personal conduct

Ms. Hertz has failed to fully cooperate with the human resources department and her department head in regard to a personal relationship that she has developed with a staff member under her supervision.

I refer to a January 18, 20xx, memo to file about Ms. Hertz's personal relationship with a member of her staff. According to the head of her department, although supervisory responsibility for Mr. X was transferred to another manager, Ms. Hertz has apparently shown special favoritism in assignments and work hours for Mr. X.

This situation is an apparent violation of the rules set forth in the employee manual.

We have made it clear to Ms. Hertz that we value her commitment to the organization and her work very highly. We want to see her succeed and have every opportunity for further advancement, and we respect her right to privacy outside of the workplace. The only reason for our involvement in a personal matter such as this is to seek to avoid complications that can arise when there is a relationship between a supervisor and an employee that goes beyond the office setting.

With this memo, I am directing Ms. Hertz to end any such special treatment for Mr. X or anyone else in her department with whom she may have a personal relationship. I have asked her departmental head and the director of the human resources department to report to me within ten days about the status of this situation.

In the event that this issue is not resolved at that time in accordance with the employee manual, we will consider reassignment of Ms. Hertz to a nonmanagerial job, if one is available, or seek her termination from employment.

Confidential: Personnel matter
Date: April 1, 20xx
Manager:
Regarding employee: Katie Hertz
Subject: Personal conduct

I am writing to inform you that according to the reports of the director of the human resources department and your department head, you have failed to meet expectations in dealing with a personal relationship that you acknowledge that you have developed with a staff member under your supervision.

I refer to a January 18, 20xx, memo to file about your personal relationship with a member of your staff. According to new reports received by me on this date, although supervisory responsibility for Mr. X was transferred to another manager, you have apparently shown special favoritism in assignments and work hours for Mr. X.

This situation is an apparent violation of the rules set forth in the employee manual.

We have made it clear that we value your commitment to the organization and your work very highly. We want to see you succeed and have every opportunity for further advancement. In addition, we respect your right to privacy outside of the workplace. The only reason for our involvement in a personal matter such as this is to seek to avoid complications that can arise when there is a relationship between a supervisor and an employee that goes beyond the office setting.

With this memo, I am directing you to end any such special treatment for Mr. X or anyone else in your department with whom you may have a personal relationship. I have asked your departmental head and the director of the human resources department to report to me within ten days about the status of this situation.

In the event that this issue is not resolved at that time in accordance with the employee manual, we will consider reassigning you to a nonmanagerial job, if one is available, or seeking your termination from employment.

Quid Pro Quo

Perhaps the most treacherous territory in the workplace is the ground trod by practitioners and victims of a sexual quid pro quo. This is a very serious risk to the organization and in many cases the accused employee. Be sure to involve the in-house attorney or an outside counsel in all aspects of responding to any accusation, confession, or evidence of this sort of activity.

Earlier in this chapter we outlined the general steps that need to be followed in acknowledging and documenting such claims. We will leave this particular category to be handled under the guidance of appropriate legal counsel.

Chapter 7

LAW AND ORDER

NO ONE IS above the law, including individuals, organizations, government agencies, educational institutions, and corporations.

If someone is accused of breaking a regulation or law that relates entirely to their personal life, and if that infraction takes place away from the workplace and has nothing to do with an individual's job or employment status, that could be a situation in which the employer has no liability or involvement. An example would be an employee who, while driving his own car on the weekend, is involved in an automobile accident and ticketed for excessive speed.

Still, the fact is that almost everything an employee does on or off the job can become a matter of concern for an employer.

Here are some situations to consider:

- If an employee is involved in an automobile accident while on a company assignment (whether in his own auto, a company vehicle, or a rental car), liability may extend to the organization.
- If an employer is aware (or, within the bounds of the law, should be aware) that an employee has a health or medical condition or a substance abuse problem, and that employee becomes involved in an accident, the organization's level of exposure may rise.

- If an employee has a criminal record or a past history of civil judgments and is accused of violating the law in a similar manner while representing the organization, liability may be increased.

A WORD *to the* WISE

This is an area of potentially serious legal jeopardy. Be sure to involve your in-house or outside legal counsel for advice before proceeding with any action.

These are only a few examples of legal exposure for employers. Recent accounting scandals and misconduct by boards of directors of publicly held companies have brought about laws like the Sarbanes-Oxley Act (the Public Company Accounting Reform and Investor Protection Act) as well as stiffened regulations by stock exchanges, state regulatory boards, and government agencies.

The upshot is that in general, employees as well as their supervisors and managers are responsible not only for following laws and regulations (maintaining compliance) but also for producing and keeping on file an audit trail that proves that every safeguard has been followed.

At the same time, regulations intended to safeguard privacy place limits on what the organization has the right to insist on knowing about the activities—or legal entanglements—of its employees that happen away from the workplace. What's the bottom line? If you become aware of a situation that has occurred off the clock, away from the workplace and in an employee's private life, contact human resources or your in-house or outside counsel before making any further inquiries or taking any actions.

Criminal Law and Civil Lawsuits

As we have noted, any time there is a hint of a lawsuit or a referral to an outside legal or regulatory agency that is in any way related to the company or organization's property or while an employee is representing the organization, you should immediately involve your organization's in-house or outside counsel. We are not attorneys, and even if we were, there are so many landmines to avoid that we could not possibly offer blanket advice in this book.

If you suspect a problem, receive an allegation of illegality, or see evidence of wrongdoing, do the following:

1. If there is an ongoing threat to safety, immediately contact police, fire, or medical authorities. After doing so, follow any further instructions in the employee manual or in other training you may have received.
2. If someone has been injured, immediately contact the appropriate emergency response agency: the police, an ambulance service, or in-house medical staff. Don't call a supervisor or a lawyer first; notify these people after help has been summoned.
3. If someone has committed a crime of violence or has caused someone to be injured, immediately contact the police. Notify supervisors and lawyers after help has been summoned.
4. If it appears that theft, fraud, or other nonviolent laws may have been broken, contact your in-house

or outside counsel immediately and follow their instructions.

5. Don't touch, remove, or alter evidence in any way.

6. Seek the advice of legal counsel and follow instructions as to whether you should take any written notes, make photographs, or do anything other than provide immediate assistance to anyone who has been injured. In general, your best course of action is to take notes on anything there is to be seen and on anything you are told or directly overhear. Beyond that, don't ask questions other than those necessary to summon emergency services.

7. Follow any other guidelines that are part of the employee manual or any training you may have received from in-house or outside legal counsel.

The bottom line is that you want to be able to say that you did everything possible to assist anyone who was injured on the job and that you notified proper authorities of any possible illegality as quickly as possible. You don't want to have to explain to a police officer, a plaintiff, an outside agency, or a judge why you did something to delay assistance, impede an investigation, or avoid consequences. You also do not want to have to explain why you asked questions that moved into matters of privacy.

Unaccountable

Derek Klein is very capable when it comes to crunching the numbers. He knows his job description, understands the organization and its mission statement, and rarely makes an error. He keeps current on the latest IRS tax rulings and codes.

When it comes to following the letter of the law, though, Klein prefers to blaze his own path. As far as management and outside auditors are concerned, his work is accurate and correct, but when it comes to the details of compliance, Mr. Klein loses his concentration.

According to the law and the components of his job description, Mr. Klein is supposed to notate in his personal online calendar and in a special software program that marks compliance waypoints and deadlines and leaves an audit trail for legal and accounting purposes. But he has not consistently done so.

Verbal Notification

I have asked you to meet with me to review our current requirements to maintain a record of compliance with federal and state regulations.

I want to assure you that we consider you a very capable and valued employee and hope to see you experience continued success within the organization. The quality of your accounting work is not in question here.

However, we do have concerns that you are not fully following specified procedures to maintain records of compliance with all regulations. As you know, we have installed a computer-based calendar and database that verifies each step in a compliance procedure and adds a timestamp and employee name. You received training on the use of this program six months ago, and you were instructed at that time that its use was now an element of your job description.

I am informed, though, that you have not made regular use of the program. Is there a reason why you have not done so? Do you require some additional training? Is there some other problem I should know about?

MEMO TO FILE: Noting a request for action

Confidential: Personnel matter
Date: January 15, 20xx
Manager:
Regarding employee: Derek Klein
Subject: Audit trail procedure

I met today with Mr. Klein to review our current requirements to maintain a record of compliance with federal and state regulations and to express our concerns that he has not been fully following specified procedures to maintain records of compliance with all regulations.

I reviewed the fact that the organization is committed to following all applicable federal and state laws and regulations. As part of that commitment, we have installed a computer-based calendar and database that verifies each step in a compliance procedure and adds a timestamp and employee name.

Mr. Klein received training on use of this program six months ago and was instructed at that time that its use was now an element of his job description.

I assured Mr. Klein that we consider him a very capable and valued employee and hope to see him experience continued success within the organization. However, we cannot permit employees to ignore or violate laws and regulations related to our business, and we expect full cooperation when it comes to maintaining an audit trail where we direct one be recorded.

Mr. Klein told me he felt the compliance software was difficult to use and did not match his style of work. I reminded him that its use had been made an element of his job description. We agreed that he would receive additional training.

MEMO TO FILE: Offer of assistance

Confidential: Personnel matter
Date: January 18, 20xx
Manager:
Regarding employee: Derek Klein
Subject: Audit trail procedure

I have today received an outline from the human resources department of a four-day training program that has been developed for Mr. Klein to assist him in the use of the computer-based compliance management system.

In a meeting on January 15, I reviewed with Mr. Klein our current requirements to maintain a record of compliance with federal and state regulations and to express our concerns that he has not been fully following specified procedures to maintain records of compliance with all regulations. Use of the compliance management system was added to Mr. Klein's job description six months ago.

Mr. Klein agreed to take the additional training and to make use of the compliance software as directed. I have asked the human resources department to advise me of his progress in the training, which is scheduled to begin within one week. I have also requested that Mr. Klein's department head report back to me in thirty days on the status of this issue.

PERFORMANCE EVALUATION: Acknowledging progress

Confidential: Personnel matter
Date: April 1, 20xx
Manager:
Regarding employee: Derek Klein
Subject: Audit trail procedure

I am informed by the human resources department and by Mr. Klein's department head that he successfully completed a training course on the compliance management software now in use in the organization. Further, I am informed that Mr. Klein has been using the software as directed.

PERFORMANCE EVALUATION: Fails to meet expectations

Confidential: Personnel matter
Date: April 1, 20xx
Manager:
Regarding employee: Derek Klein
Subject: Audit trail procedure

I am informed that Mr. Klein continues to fail to meet our expectations in the use of the compliance management software now required as part of his job description.

This issue first came to my attention in January. (See memos and performance evaluations dated January 15 and January 18.) At that time, Mr. Klein was instructed to take a specialized training course developed by the human resources department. Although he did complete the training, I am informed that he has not consistently followed instructions in recording accounting and financial data and reports.

With this performance evaluation, as per the employee manual, I am notifying Mr. Klein that I will meet with his supervisor in fifteen days, on April 16, to formally review his work product. If at that time it is determined that there has been no significant progress toward meeting the expectations of his job description—including use of the compliance management software for all appropriate tasks—we will consider offering a transfer to another job we feel is better suited to his skills or a termination of employment.

WRITTEN WARNING

Confidential: Personnel matter
Date: April 1, 20xx
Manager:
Regarding employee: Derek Klein
Subject: Audit trail procedure

I am writing to notify you that I will meet with your department head in fifteen days, on April 16, to formally review your work product. If at that time it is determined that there has been no significant progress toward meeting the expectations of your job description—including use of the compliance management software for all appropriate tasks—we will consider either offering a transfer to another job we feel is better suited to your skills or terminating your employment.

Ex Post Facto

As the organization's regulatory compliance officer, Paul Rooney exists in a constant state of panic. His year is made up of a hundred deadlines large and small, and by the very nature of his job he has several layers of outsiders who are constantly looking over his shoulder at his work product.

Among his tasks is making sure that all appropriate employees receive training on matters related to two key federal mandates: the Americans with Disabilities Act and the establishment and maintenance of an audit trail for provisions of the Sarbanes-Oxley Act.

Although the quality and accuracy of his work are not in question, there have been several instances in which government agencies or outside auditors have issued notices of checkpoints that were missed or appear to have been post-dated. Although the organization has not faced a formal complaint or regulatory action, there is concern from in-house counsel that there is the possibility of exposure in the event of a legal action.

Verbal Notification

I've asked you to meet with me to discuss a potential problem we would like to avoid. According to your department head and immediate supervisor, you have not met targets for training and compliance audits for many of the projects for which you are responsible.

We value you as an employee and want to see that you have success in the organization. However, we cannot permit these important benchmarks to be ignored. This organization is fully committed to compliance with all applicable federal and state laws and regulations.

Your primary assignment, as stated in your job description, is to make certain that all supervisors receive training on the provisions of the Americans with Disabilities Act and the Sarbanes-Oxley Act. Specifically, we expect to see complete and accurate records reflecting such training as well as in-service monitoring.

It has been brought to my attention by two of your supervisors that several documents related to financial disclosure forms appear to have been filed well past the mandated deadline. In at least one case, the forms were post-dated as if they had been filed on time, but computer records indicate they were entered into the compliance software thirty days late. I am sure you are aware that it is essential we avoid even the perception of impropriety in all our legal obligations.

Is there a particular reason why you seem to be having problems meeting your targets and goals?

MEMO TO FILE: Noting a request for action

Confidential: Personnel matter
Date: January 15, 20xx
Manager:
Regarding employee: Paul Rooney
Subject: Training requirements

I met today with Mr. Rooney to discuss a potential problem we would like to avoid. According to his department head and immediate supervisor, Mr. Rooney has not met targets for training and compliance audits for many of the projects for which he is responsible.

I assured Mr. Rooney that we value him as an employee and want to see that he has success in the organization. However, I reiterated that we cannot permit these important benchmarks to be ignored. This organization is fully committed to compliance with all applicable federal and state laws and regulations.

As stated in the job description, Mr. Rooney's primary assignment is to make certain that all supervisors receive training on the provisions of the Americans with Disabilities Act and the Sarbanes-Oxley Act. Specifically, we expect to see complete and accurate records reflecting such training as well as in-service monitoring.

It has been brought to my attention by two of Mr. Rooney's supervisors that several documents related to financial disclosure forms appear to have been filed well past the mandated deadline. In at least one case, the forms were post-dated as if they had been filed on time, but computer records indicate they were entered into the compliance software thirty days late.

I advised Mr. Rooney that is essential we avoid even the perception of impropriety in all our legal obligations.

I asked Mr. Rooney if there was a particular reason why he seems to be having problems meeting targets and goals. In response, he said that he felt overwhelmed by the number of tasks in his job description.

I have requested that Mr. Rooney meet with his department head, his supervisor, and a representative of the human resources department to discuss possible modifications to his job description. This meeting is to take place within ten days, and I expect a report on the status of this issue within fifteen days.

MEMO TO FILE: Offer of assistance

Confidential: Personnel matter
Date: January 28, 20xx
Manager:
Regarding employee: Paul Rooney
Subject: Training requirements

I met today with Mr. Rooney and his supervisor to discuss a proposal to restructure his job description. Based on recommendations from the human resources department, we have decided to assign Mr. Rooney to concentrate on monitoring compliance with the Sarbanes-Oxley financial regulations and to transfer oversight of Americans with Disabilities Act (ADA) compliance to another member of staff.

It was agreed that the growing demands of Sarbanes-Oxley regulations had reached the point where Mr. Rooney was unable to devote sufficient attention to that task as well as ADA issues.

I have made it clear to Mr. Rooney that with this adjustment in his job description, we expect to see complete and accurate records reflecting such training as well as in-service monitoring. We will expect that all reports and audits will be filed on or before deadlines from this point forward.

I have asked Mr. Rooney's supervisor for an update in thirty days and again in sixty days on progress in meeting job goals.

PERFORMANCE EVALUATION: Acknowledging progress

Confidential: Personnel matter
Date: April 1, 20xx
Manager:
Regarding employee: Paul Rooney
Subject: Training requirements

I have been advised by Mr. Rooney's supervisor that since his job description was changed in mid-January to concentrate on Sarbanes-Oxley financial compliance issues, Mr. Rooney has met all expectations in filing reports and audits on time and with full detail.

It is apparent that Mr. Rooney's previous job description was too broad in its scope. We appreciate his good efforts in recent weeks.

PERFORMANCE EVALUATION: Fails to meet expectations

Confidential: Personnel matter
Date: April 1, 20xx
Manager:
Regarding employee: Paul Rooney
Subject: Training requirements

I have been advised by Mr. Rooney's supervisor that although his job description was changed in mid-January to concentrate on Sarbanes-Oxley financial compliance issues, Mr. Rooney has continued to fail to meet expectations in filing reports and audits on time and with full detail.

Based on recommendations from the human resources department, we decided in January to assign Mr. Rooney to concentrate on monitoring compliance with the Sarbanes-Oxley financial regulations and to transfer oversight of Americans with Disabilities Act (ADA) compliance to another member of staff.

It was felt that the growing demands of Sarbanes-Oxley regulations had reached the point where Mr. Rooney was unable to devote sufficient attention to that task as well as ADA issues.

However, we now find that despite this adjustment in his job description, Mr. Rooney has not been able to provide complete and accurate records reflecting such training as well as in-service monitoring.

With this performance evaluation, as per the employee manual, I am notifying Mr. Rooney that I will meet with his supervisor in fifteen days to formally review his work product. If at that time it is determined that there has been no significant progress toward meeting the expectations of his job description, we will consider either offering a transfer to another job we feel is better suited to his skills or terminating his employment.

Confidential: Personnel matter
Date: April 1, 20xx
Manager:
Regarding employee: Paul Rooney
Subject: Training requirements

I am writing to notify you that I will meet with your department head in fifteen days to formally review your work product. If at that time it is determined that there has been no significant progress toward meeting the expectations of your job description, we will consider either offering a transfer to another job we feel is better suited to your skills or terminating your employment.

The Police Come Calling

Pete Smith and Olmeda Jones don't like each other. They don't have to be friends, either. They work in different departments and have no official interaction on any level within the organization.

But if they happen to pass each other in the hall or see each other on their own time in a shopping mall, those around them know to expect rolling eyes, sneers and smirks, and the occasional muttered insult.

It all existed below the radar of upper management, and in truth, had no bearing on either man's productivity in the organization. That is, until one day the police came calling. Mr. Smith had phoned in a complaint alleging Mr. Jones had made a threat against him and his family after a verbal altercation in the employee parking lot. In this section, we are going to concentrate on Mr. Jones, who is alleged to have made the threat. A similar process would go on with Mr. Smith.

Verbal Notification

I've asked you to meet with me to discuss the recent incident regarding you and Mr. Smith.

I do not have all of the facts. I have asked the human resources department to manage an investigation that will include the police report, statements by you, by Mr. Smith, and any witnesses. In addition, they will be speaking with your supervisor and department head.

We value you as an employee and hope for your success with the organization. However, you must understand that we consider any acts of violence, harassment, or threats of violence to be a most serious breach of the employee code of conduct and grounds for immediate termination.

While we investigate this situation and until we have determined the facts, we are suspending you from your job. I want you to go to the human resources department immediately and discuss the terms of that suspension and your rights and obligations.

Is this clear to you?

MEMO TO FILE: Noting a request for action

Confidential: Personnel matter
Date: January 15, 20xx
Manager:
Regarding employee: Olmeda Jones
Subject: Personal conduct

I met today with Mr. Jones to discuss the recent incident regarding Mr. Jones and Mr. Smith that resulted in a police investigation of an alleged threat. A copy of the official report is on file in the human resources department.

I have asked human resources to manage an investigation that will include the police report, statements by Mr. Jones, by Mr. Smith, and any witnesses. In addition, they will be speaking with the supervisor and department heads for both men.

I told Mr. Jones we value him as an employee and hope for his success with the organization. However, he must understand that we consider any acts of violence, harassment, or threats of violence to be a most serious breach of the employee code of conduct and grounds for immediate termination.

While we investigate this situation and until we have determined the facts, Mr. Jones is suspended from his job. I asked him to go to the human resources department immediately and discuss the terms of that suspension and his rights and obligations.

He agreed to do so. He made no other comments about the situation.

MEMO TO FILE: Offer of assistance

Confidential: Personnel matter
Date: January 18, 20xx
Manager:
Regarding employee: Olmeda Jones
Subject: Personal conduct

I have received a report from the human resources department regarding an alleged altercation between Mr. Jones and Mr. Smith.

I have previously made it clear to Mr. Jones that we consider any acts of violence, harassment, or threats of violence to be a most serious breach of the employee code of conduct and grounds for immediate termination.

However, on the basis of a recommendation from the head of the human resources department and by Mr. Jones's department head, I have decided to allow Mr. Jones to return to his job for a probationary period.

With this memo, I am directing the human resources department to offer Mr. Jones any appropriate counseling and training that may assist him in controlling his temper and avoiding disputes with other employees.

I have asked for a report from departmental heads once a month for the next six months. If there are no further reported or observed incidents between Mr. Jones and Mr. Smith in the next six months, the probation will be lifted.

If at any time there are any further problems between these two men, or between either of them and another employee, we will move for immediate termination.

PERFORMANCE EVALUATION: Acknowledging progress

Confidential: Personnel matter
Date: July 1, 20xx
Manager:
Regarding employee: Olmeda Jones
Subject: Personal conduct

In regard to the probationary period instituted for Mr. Jones in January, I am pleased to note that his supervisor and department head report there have been no further incidents of dispute with any employee.

PERFORMANCE EVALUATION: Fails to meet expectations

Confidential: Personnel matter
Date: May 1, 20xx
Manager:
Regarding employee: Olmeda Jones
Subject: Personal conduct

I have been informed by Mr. Jones's department head that there have been several disruptive disputes between Mr. Jones and Mr. Smith in the past three weeks.

I have previously made it clear to Mr. Jones that we consider any acts of violence, harassment, or threats of violence to be a most serious breach of the employee code of conduct and grounds for immediate termination.

Effective today, Mr. Jones's employment is terminated. I have directed the human resources department to meet with him to offer any services they deem appropriate.

WRITTEN WARNING

Confidential: Personnel matter
Date: April 1, 20xx
Manager:
Regarding employee: Olmeda Jones
Subject: Personal conduct

Based on an investigation by the human resources department, we have determined that you once again engaged in a heated verbal dispute with Mr. Smith.

I have previously made it clear that we consider any acts of violence, harassment, or threats of violence to be a most serious breach of the employee code of conduct and grounds for immediate termination.

Effective today, your employment is terminated.

I have asked the human resources department to make available any counseling or services that they deem appropriate.

Chapter 8

SUBSTANCE ABUSE

ALCOHOL AND DRUGS are a fact of life. When it comes to their use and abuse in the personal lives of employees, they can become a matter of concern, causing absenteeism as well as medical and psychological issues. If they are used while an employee is in the workplace, they can lead to serious problems in productivity and quality of work, interpersonal relationships, and liability in case of an accident or incident. Finally, problems with substance abuse raise the cost of health benefits for the entire enterprise.

Because alcohol and drugs can affect an organization's ability to perform its mission, interfere with its relations with suppliers and clients, and cause disruption in the workplace, it is generally within the employer's right to establish reasonable rules that apply equally to all employees.

Some federal and state governments require the establishment of drug-free workplaces as conditions for contracts. In unionized workplaces, the subject of mandatory testing is usually an element of collective bargaining agreements.

At the same time, many organizations sincerely want to be able to tell their employees that they are part of a "family" and offer support and programs to help them get out from under an addiction or substance abuse.

The leading problematic substance is alcohol. By some estimates, 10 million people in the United States are "alcohol-dependent"; in the workforce, that may equate to about one in ten who have some level of problem.

Drug use, ranging from prescription drug abuse to marijuana to narcotics, affects about 8 percent of the American population, or about one in twelve.

Elements of a Substance Abuse Policy

A substance abuse program has to navigate a course between some significant legal landmines—the right to privacy, the presumption of innocence, and general employment law being just a few. Be sure to consult with your in-house attorney or outside counsel in the creation, implementation, and enforcement of any drug abuse policy in the workplace.

Here are some general components of a typical written policy that is part of the employee handbook, job description, or special training given to staff and supervisors:

1. An extension of the organization's mission statement that explains why alcohol or drug abuse presents a problem for the employer, employee, and clients.

2. Details of training programs offered to supervisors and human resources personnel on dealing with employees with substance abuse problems and information about how workers are informed of company policy in this matter. Based on the advice of your attorney, the policy may institute an immediate suspension based on behavior, leaving it up to the employee to choose whether to participate in an assistance program.

3. A carefully written (and attorney-vetted) discussion of the means by which the organization can identify substance abusers. Certain types of jobs, including those involving transportation services, operators of hazardous equipment, or handlers of dangerous chemicals, may require that the employee submit to scheduled or random testing. Jobs that involve the management of sensitive information or the handling of large amounts of cash or other valuables may also be included in some descriptions. The employer may be permitted to insist on a test in the aftermath of an accident. The employer may be able to insist on testing if an employee demonstrates specific types of behavior in the workplace.

4. Details of the process for drug testing, along with the nature of substances that are included in the program.

5. Statement of the organization's right to inspect lockers, storage areas, desks, its owned or leased vehicles, and other facilities on a scheduled or unannounced basis. Consult with an attorney before conducting a search of individuals.

6. A description of the sort of help (often called an employee assistance program) that will be offered to staffers who are identified as substance abusers or who voluntarily report their situation.

7. Specific details of the sanctions that will be applied for violation of substance abuse policies. In most organizations, the process begins with a referral to an outside medical agency for assessment with a requirement that specific goals are accomplished.

8. Assertion of the employer's right to terminate an employee for failure to cooperate with substance abuse programs or for specific repeat violations of policies.

It is important for an employer to take into account the fact that certain health conditions or prescription medications may affect performance or behavior in the workplace. Some legal medications may also cause incorrect results on drug tests.

Employers have the right to require notification of medical conditions that may affect the ability of a staffer to perform his or her duties properly or safely. At the same time, the Americans with Disabilities Act (ADA) and other federal and state legislation generally bar an employer from discrimination in hiring and firing practices based on use of legal medications. The ADA makes it illegal to ask questions about disabilities, medical conditions, and medications unless there is a specific relation to a job. The areas of danger for the employer and employee usually involve hazardous jobs.

Consult with an attorney before taking any action regarding an employee because of effects of a medication.

What Should the Employer Know?

Here are some excerpts from a typical application for employment:

Have you ever been convicted of a crime other than a minor traffic violation? "Convicted" means you were declared guilty by a judge or you pleaded guilty in court to a charge that is either a misdemeanor or a felony. In certain legal proceedings, a person may be convicted of a crime but not required to pay a fine or penalty, or spend time in jail or in prison.

Traffic violations that are usually not considered minor include driving while under the influence of alcohol or drugs, operating a motor vehicle without a driver's license or with a suspended license, leaving the scene of an accident, or committing a moving violation that causes injury or death.

In applying for this job, you give permission to the employer to conduct a criminal history investigation. You understand that if you are offered employment before such an investigation is completed, your employment is conditional, subject to the findings.

A criminal record does not automatically disqualify you for employment. The employer reserves the right to decide whether past legal problems are relevant to the job. However, falsification of any responses on the application will always disqualify an applicant, regardless of how well qualified.

Here is language from an employee manual that relates to events that might occur after someone is on the payroll:

Some offenses that take place on or off company property, during work hours or when the employee is not at work, are considered sufficiently serious to result in immediate termination. These include acts of violence, the carrying of weapons of any sort in the workplace, or possession of any illegal weapon away from the workplace. Other unacceptable violations are the possession, use, sale, purchase, or distribution of any illegal drug or substance. Also considered serious violations are theft, breaches of confidentiality, and falsification of records. This list is by no means complete. The organization reserves the right to terminate an employee for other offenses.

Further, the human resources department will consider the facts of an arrest, criminal complaint, summons to answer a criminal charge, indictment, or any other criminal charge or conviction as the basis for disciplinary action including suspension or termination.

Employees are required to report any arrests, indictments, or convictions to the human resources department within twenty-four hours after they occur during the workweek, or on the first business day after they occur.

Do not adopt this example of an employee manual for use in your own company or organization without seeking review by an attorney.

A WORD *to the* WISE

An employee, like any citizen, is presumed innocent until proven guilty. An employer who makes an allegation of criminality or violation of civil law—in the absence of a finding by a court, a government agency, or other legal entity—runs the risk of a claim of defamation by the employee. Be sure to involve your in-house or outside counsel before making any allegations of illegality or making any actions based on a belief of violation of the law.

Hung Over

There comes a point at which a snicker becomes a concern and eventually an issue. That's the story with Jean Janus, the front-desk receptionist.

At first, Ms. Janus was a source of entertainment for some of the staff when she would show up on Mondays with dark circles below her eyes, a bottle of aspirin, and—with just a tiny bit of nudging—a story of the morning after the night before. Through her gauzy haze, she nevertheless managed to answer the phone and greet visitors.

But lately Mondays have reached into Tuesdays and Wednesdays, and TGIF seems to be arriving on Thursday. What began as a mild joke in the workplace has become unsettling to many coworkers and noticed by visitors and callers.

Verbal Notification

Jean, I've asked you to meet with me to discuss a matter of personal behavior that has begun to affect your ability to perform your job as a receptionist.

We value you as an employee and hope to see you succeed in your current assignment and other positions in the future. However, we are concerned that activities taking place in your private life are affecting your performance at the reception desk. As outlined in the job description, we expect you to dress in a business-like style, be alert and effective in screening and assisting visitors, and overall to behave in a professional manner.

We have received a number of reports from visitors and employees that in recent weeks you have appeared hung over or intoxicated on the job. Neither condition is acceptable for an employee in your position.

Is there anything you want to tell me that might explain these observations of your behavior?

Is there anything we can do as an organization to help you perform your assigned duties?

MEMO TO FILE: Noting a request for action

Confidential: Personnel matter
Date: January 15, 20xx
Manager:
Regarding employee: Jean Janus
Subject: Personal conduct

I met today with Ms. Janus to discuss a matter of personal behavior that in the judgment of her supervisor has begun to affect her ability to perform her job as a receptionist.

I emphasized to Ms. Janus that we value her as an employee and hope to see her succeed in her current assignment and other positions in the future. However, I explained to her that we are concerned that activities taking place in her private life are affecting her performance at the reception desk.

We have received a number of reports from visitors and employees that in recent weeks Ms. Janus has appeared hung over or intoxicated on the job. I told her that neither condition is acceptable for an employee in her position.

I reviewed some of the elements of the job description for receptionist, including the expectation that she dress in a business-like style, be alert and effective in screening and assisting visitors, and overall behave in a professional manner.

I asked Ms. Janus if there was anything she wanted to tell me that might explain these observations of her behavior. I also asked if there was anything we could do as an organization to help her perform her assigned duties.

In response, Ms. Janus asked to meet in private with a representative of the human resources department to learn about offerings in the employee assistance program (EAP). I told her I would arrange for someone else to cover her station for the remainder of the day, and I set up an immediate meeting with the EAP supervisor.

MEMO TO FILE: Offer of assistance

Confidential: Personnel matter
Date: January 18, 20xx
Manager:
Regarding employee: Jean Janus
Subject: Personal conduct

According to a confidential memo received on this date from the human resources department, Jean Janus has requested support from the employee assistance program (EAP).

In keeping with our policy, the EAP and the human resources department manager will offer whatever counseling, medical, or special services they deem appropriate.

I will receive a progress report from the human resources department on February 1 and again on the first business day of each month for as long as that department feels necessary. The report will deal only with specific behavior that occurs in the workplace, as identified in the memo to file of January 15, 20xx. It is our policy and intention to protect private medical records from unauthorized viewing, and such information will not be included in the reports I receive.

PERFORMANCE EVALUATION: Acknowledging progress

Confidential: Personnel matter
Date: April 1, 20xx
Manager:
Regarding employee: Jean Janus
Subject: Personal conduct

We have noted a significant improvement in performance by Ms. Janus in the past six weeks since she began working with the employee assistance program. We hope to see continued progress on the issues first identified in January of this year.

I have asked for a continuation of monthly reports from the human resources department and from Ms. Janus's supervisor.

PERFORMANCE EVALUATION: Fails to meet expectations

Confidential: Personnel matter
Date: April 1, 20xx
Manager:
Regarding employee: Jean Janus
Subject: Personal conduct

I am informed by the human resources department and by her immediate supervisor that the issues of personal conduct with Ms. Janus first identified in January of this year have not been resolved.

On January 18, 20xx, I directed the human resources department to engage the employee assistance program and offer all appropriate services to Ms. Janus. The nature of their findings and the particular services offered to Ms. Janus are considered confidential and are not specifically identified in this performance evaluation.

With this evaluation, I am informing Ms. Janus that unless her on-the-job performance and demeanor improve significantly in the next fifteen days, we may choose to reassign her to another position, if available, or seek her immediate termination from employment.

WRITTEN WARNING

Confidential: Personnel matter
Date: April 1, 20xx
Manager:
Regarding employee: Jean Janus
Subject: Personal conduct

I am writing to inform you that based on confidential reports from the human resources department and by your immediate supervisor, we feel that the issues of personal conduct first identified in January of this year have not been resolved.

On January 18, 20xx, I directed the human resources department to engage the employee assistance program and offer you all appropriate services. The nature of findings and the particular services offered are considered confidential and are not included in your performance evaluation record.

Once again, I want to emphasize to you that we value you as an employee and hope to see you succeed in your current assignment and other positions in the future.

However, with this evaluation, I am informing you that unless your on-the-job performance and demeanor improves significantly in the next fifteen days, we may choose to reassign you to another position, if available, or seek your immediate termination from employment.

The Loose Wheel

When Lucy Guise was hired as a delivery driver, she had a clean driving record, and on her job application she advised her employer of that fact. As part of the hiring process, the human resources department verified her record with the Department of Motor Vehicles.

But that was three years ago, and in the meantime she has racked up two speeding tickets and three moving violations, and she was arrested and charged with driving while under the influence of alcohol. All this happened on her own time, while she was using her personal vehicle.

A WORD *to the* WISE

Be sure that any language in your organization's employee manual regarding arrests and convictions, as well as any requirement for notification of the employer, has been approved by a capable employment attorney.

Ms. Guise hired an attorney who managed to have the DUI charge reduced to excessive speed.

She reported none of this to her supervisor, and none of it would have come to her employer's attention except for one seemingly insignificant event: One day, while making a delivery using a company vehicle, she was involved in a minor fender-bender. There were no injuries, and the police report blamed the accident on the other driver. But the company's insurance company, investigating the accident before paying a claim, uncovered Ms. Guise's personal driving record. They reported what they found to her employer and indicated their intention to re-rate the cost of coverage because the company was permitting drivers with unsafe records to operate its vehicles.

Verbal Notification

I've asked you to meet with me to discuss an apparent violation of company policy. As a member of our transportation department, you are required to report any arrests or convictions related to your driving record, as well as any non-minor traffic violations. This applies to both events that may happen while you are using a company vehicle or on your own time in your own vehicle.

This was made clear to you when you applied for a job, and it is an element of your job description.

I am aware that you had a minor non-injury accident with a company truck two weeks ago. Our insurance company has informed me that in their investigation of the claim, they found that over the past three years you have been stopped by the police for several serious traffic violations while driving your personal vehicle. According to their report, these include two speeding tickets, three moving violations, and driving while under the influence of alcohol.

Our company policy is very straightforward. While we investigate this situation and until we have verified the facts, we are suspending you from your job. I want you to go to the human resources department immediately and discuss the terms of that suspension and your rights and obligations.

Is this clear to you?

MEMO TO FILE: Noting a request for action

Confidential: Personnel matter
Date: January 15, 20xx
Manager:
Regarding employee: Lucy Guise
Subject: Transportation department regulations

I met today with Ms. Guise to discuss an apparent violation of company policy. As a member of our transportation department, Ms. Guise is required to report any arrests or convictions related to her driving record, as well as any non-minor traffic violations. This applies to events that may happen either while she is using a company vehicle or while she was on her own time in her own vehicle.

This is an important element of the pre-employment interview, and it is included in the job description.

I told Ms. Guise that as a result of a minor non-injury accident that occurred while she was driving a company truck two weeks ago, our insurance company has contacted us. In their investigation of the claim, the insurance company reports that they found that over the past three years, Ms. Guise has been stopped by the police for several serious traffic violations while driving her personal vehicle. According to their report, these include two speeding tickets, three moving violations, and driving while under the influence of alcohol.

In keeping with company policy, I have immediately suspended Ms. Guise from her job while we investigate this situation and verify the facts.

I asked Ms. Guise to go to the human resources department immediately and discuss the terms of that suspension and her rights and obligations.

I asked Ms. Guise if everything I had said was clear to her. She said she understood. She went on to say that her lawyer had told her that she did not have to inform us of the DUI arrest because it had been reduced to a charge of excessive speed. When I began taking notes she said, "I don't think I should say anything more until I speak with my attorney."

I have asked the human resources department to keep me informed of the status of their investigation and to advise me on any further personnel procedures that need to be taken.

PERFORMANCE EVALUATION: Fails to meet expectations

Confidential: Personnel matter
Date: February 1, 20xx
Manager:
Regarding employee: Lucy Guise
Subject: Transportation department regulations

Based on an investigation by the human resources department, we have verified that Ms. Guise has violated company policy at least five times in the past three years. During that period, she failed to notify us of stops for non-minor traffic offenses including two speeding tickets, three moving violations, and driving while under the influence of alcohol.

As a member of our transportation department, Ms. Guise is required to report any arrests or convictions related to her driving record, as well as any non-minor traffic violations. This applies to events that may happen either while she is using a company vehicle or while she is on her own time in her own vehicle. This is an important element of the pre-employment interview, and it is included in the job description.

Effective today, Ms. Guise's employment is terminated.

WRITTEN NOTIFICATION

Confidential: Personnel matter
Date: February 1, 20xx
Manager:
Regarding employee: Lucy Guise
Subject: Transportation department regulations

Based on an investigation by the human resources department, we have verified that you have violated company policy at least five times in the past three years. During that period you have failed to notify us of arrests for non-minor traffic offenses including two speeding tickets, three moving violations, and driving while under the influence of alcohol.

As a member of our transportation department, you are required to report any arrests or convictions related to your driving record, as well as any non-minor traffic violations. This applies to events that may happen either while you are using a company vehicle or while you are on your own time in your own vehicle. This is an important element of the pre-employment interview and it is included in the job description.

Effective today, your employment is terminated.

I have asked the human resources department to make available any counseling or services that they deem appropriate.

Chapter 9

DISCRIMINATION

LET'S START WITH the bottom line: If you make a personnel or policy decision based on who someone is rather than how that person performs his or her job, you may be in violation of one or more federal, state, or local laws.

As a manager, if you countenance, permit, or ignore discrimination—or if you don't take seriously any allegation of discrimination, even if it is frivolous—you may be putting yourself and your organization at risk as well.

Just as it is often not the crime but the cover-up that gets politicians, businesspeople, and ordinary citizens into trouble, mistreating a claim of discrimination is an invitation for complaints, unrest, lawsuits, or action by government agencies. All are things best avoided.

Although the principles of equality and fairness were broadly painted in the Bill of Rights that accompanies the U.S. Constitution, the basis of current antidiscrimination law comes from the civil rights movement of the 1960s and the landmark federal Civil Rights Act of 1964. Title VII of that law and subsequent amendments and extensions make it illegal to do any of the following on the basis of someone's race, ethnic or national origin, gender, or religion:

- Refuse to hire
- Fire
- Take disciplinary action

- Fail to offer training or other assistance
- Demote or fail to promote
- Pay less than others in the same job
- Harass

It is also illegal to set up a hiring policy or rules and regulations for workers already on the job that have the effect of discriminating against a particular class of people. You can't, for example, demand that all secretaries be women (or even worse, young women of particular physical attributes), and you can't institute a test for hiring or promotion that tends to exclude (or specify) persons of color.

There are exceptions, though. Lawyers and human resources departments often cite strength tests for firefighters. Although this may tend to exclude most women and those with certain physical handicaps, if the job description legitimately requires that the employee be able to carry heavy equipment or victims, passing the test can be required. However, the test cannot be constructed in a way intended to exclude women (or any other protected class) and must be realistic. You can't require an applicant to lift seventy-five pounds if the heaviest weight an employee will have to bear is fifty pounds.

Other exceptions that have been upheld include requirements that attendants in a women's locker room be female or that certain jobs in religious organizations be filled by believers. Some clever lawyers have found ways to permit their clients to hire only women or men as wait staff or entertainers in places where clients expect such attributes.

The key here is that antidiscrimination law only applies when an employer takes an action based on a person's protected status (race, sex, religion, age, origin, or disability) as opposed to reasonably defined job requirements.

A WORD *to the* WISE

We're not lawyers, and this is not intended as legal advice. If you have any doubt about how to handle a hiring, disciplinary, or termination issue, you should seek the assistance of your company or institution's legal counsel.

Most of the federal laws that make "sex" a protected class do not provide full protection to sexual orientation. However, a number of states have extended the law to make homosexuality a protected class. Because this is a gray area, tread carefully here.

Most of the federal laws in this area are written to apply to companies and organizations of a particular size or those that engage in interstate or international commerce. State and local laws may have differing thresholds or no threshold at all. We'd strongly suggest that businesses and organizations of all sizes act as if all antidiscrimination laws apply.

Other Forms of Discrimination

As we have suggested, this is not an area where an employer or manager should work without a legal net. Seek the advice of an attorney for any questions, and take advantage of any appropriate training offered by your employer, associations, consultants, and government agencies. In this section we'll touch on some of the most important laws that apply in this area.

The federal Equal Pay Act mandates equal pay for men and women who perform equal work. It is allowable to base differences in pay on seniority or merit but not on the basis of sex. (This particular law applies to employers who come under the regulations of the Fair Labor Standards Act.)

Any employee over the age of forty is offered some protection under the federal Age Discrimination in Employment Act. Employers are generally barred from firing or forcing to retire an older worker and then hiring a younger replacement. Gray areas (pardon the pun) under this law include work practices that tend to have a positive or negative impact on workers of a particular age.

The landmark Americans with Disabilities Act (ADA) and subsequent federal legislation require employers to make "reasonable accommodation" for employees or job applicants who have disabilities. There are exceptions for jobs that require particular physical abilities.

The ADA also prohibits employers from declining to hire or discriminating against an employee whose spouse, child, or other dependent has a disability. This includes refusing to hire someone who has a family member with a disability that would impact the company or organization's health plan coverage.

Dealing with Allegations of Discrimination

The first rule of dealing with allegations of discrimination is this: Treat the individuals and the situation seriously and with respect. Listen carefully and make non-judgmental notes: date, time, the name of the person reporting a claim, and the name or names of other people who may be involved.

The second rule is this: Acknowledge the seriousness of the complaint, and give reasonable assurances that you will proceed according to the steps laid out in your organization's employee handbook.

Here's the third rule: Follow the steps. In most organizations, this means you should make immediate contact with the human resources department or the legal department or outside counsel.

Like the doctor's oath, your first responsibility is to do no harm. Don't make promises (other than acknowledging that you will follow proper procedures). Don't make judgments at this very early step in the process. Don't make things much worse by disclosing confidential information to those who have no reason to be involved or by covering up or making light of any claim.

A Hint of Trouble

Meyer Post has been with the organization for almost all of its existence, overseeing a minor but essential component that is part of an overall quality control program. He's the sort of manager who does his job, keeps out of trouble, and stays as far away from office politics as possible. No one has much to say about him one way or another except to acknowledge that he does what is expected of him.

Over the years, he has built a small department of six staffers. As with other managers, he has the final say on selection of employees once applicants have been checked and approved by human resources.

Today, out of the blue, the organization's chief personnel officer received a phone call from Mr. Jones, a recent job applicant. Mr. Jones alleged that he had not received the job because of discriminatory practices by Meyer Post. Jones gave few details but said he intended to seek assistance from a civil rights attorney if he was not offered a job with the organization.

There is nothing in Mr. Post's file to indicate that there has been a problem in the past, although as the result of inquiries from the human resources department several managers have indicated they have heard him make statements that range from racially intolerant to flat-out bigoted.

The organization's in-house counsel has been brought in to manage the case and has advised that all parties make no further oral or written comments on the situation. The lawyer hopes to resolve the problem without more formal legal filings.

Verbal Notification

I've asked you to meet with me today to discuss dealing with a possible problem related to a job applicant you dealt with recently. There may or may not be anything of concern here, but for legal reasons and the commitment of this organization to fair employment practices, we do take such matters seriously.

Because of the sensitive nature of this matter, I do not want you to go into details with me. Instead, I am directing you to immediately meet with the head of the human resources department.

MEMO TO FILE: Noting a request for action

Confidential: Personnel matter
Date: January 15, 20xx
Manager:
Regarding employee: Meyer Post
Subject: Hiring practices

I met today with Mr. Post to discuss dealing with a possible problem related to a job applicant he dealt with recently. I explained to him that there may or may not be anything of concern here, but for legal reasons and the commitment of this organization to fair employment practices, we do take such matters seriously.

I told him that because of the sensitive nature of this matter, I did not want him to go into detail with me. Instead, I asked him to immediately meet with the head of the human resources department.

MEMO TO FILE: Offer of assistance

Confidential: Personnel matter
Date: January 18, 20xx
Manager:
Regarding employee: Meyer Post
Subject: Hiring practices

According to the human resources department, there has been no finding of any improper hiring practices by Mr. Post. At the request of the department head, though, I am directing Mr. Post to undergo a three-day refresher course on hiring practices.

PERFORMANCE EVALUATION: Acknowledging progress

Confidential: Personnel matter
Date: February 1, 20xx
Manager:
Regarding employee: Meyer Post
Subject: Hiring practices

Mr. Post has successfully completed a three-day refresher course on hiring practices. The human resources department passed along their appreciation of Mr. Post's cooperation and dedication to the organization's commitment to fair hiring practices.

PERFORMANCE EVALUATION: Fails to meet expectations

Confidential: Personnel matter
Date: February 1, 20xx
Manager:
Regarding employee: Meyer Post
Subject: Hiring practices

Because of an allegation made by an applicant for employment, the human resources department and the legal department have asked that Mr. Post temporarily step aside in all matters of hiring and firing. We have made no findings about the allegation at this time. The matter continues to be under investigation by the department of human resources.

Confidential: Personnel matter
Date: March 1, 20xx
Manager:
Regarding employee: Meyer Post
Subject: Hiring practices

We have determined that you did not follow the employee code of conduct in a recent hiring decision. We take such matters very seriously, and for this reason we have decided to terminate your employment immediately.

We ask you to immediately meet with the head of the human resources department to discuss the termination process.

A Problematic Policy

There is no disguising Bob Howland's point of view. As head of the warehouse, he has never hired a woman. He doesn't think they're up to the task of handling heavy items and power equipment.

Howland knows better than to be disrespectful of job applicants or to directly state that the reason he has not offered a particular person a job is because of her sex. He just manages to always select men for the job. In fact, he always selects men who appear to be of a particular type: muscular and energetic.

Now, however, there is a problem. A recent job applicant, a young woman, has notified the human resources department that she feels she was not offered a job solely on the basis of her sex. There was no strength test, no height or weight qualifications listed in the job posting. In any case, the job applicant claims that she can handle any assignment in the warehouse without problem.

Verbal Notification

I have asked you to meet with me to discuss an allegation by a recent job applicant that she was not offered a job solely on the basis of her sex.

We have made no determination whether the allegation is true or not.

I do not want to hear any details from you about this situation.

Please do not discuss this matter with anyone else before meeting with our in-house counsel. He has directed me to send you to meet with him immediately.

MEMO TO FILE: Noting a request for action

Confidential: Personnel matter
Date: January 15, 20xx
Manager:
Regarding employee: Bob Howland
Subject: Hiring practices

I met today with Mr. Howland to discuss an allegation by a recent job applicant that she was not offered a job solely on the basis of her sex.

At this time, we have made no determination whether the allegation is true or not.

I told Mr. Howland that I did not want to hear any details from him about this situation.

Further, I instructed Mr. Howland not to discuss this matter with anyone else before meeting with our in-house counsel. I directed Mr. Howland to meet with the counsel immediately.

A WORD *to the* WISE

If a supervisor or an organization determines that an employee has likely committed a civil or criminal violation, most lawyers would advise that any disciplinary action or dismissal be handled with a simple memo stating that this is being done "in the best interests of the company." If the memo is more specific, it may end up becoming a piece of evidence in a lawsuit. In any case, be sure to discuss this sort of situation with your in-house or outside counsel before taking any action.

MEMO TO FILE: Offer of assistance

Confidential: Personnel matter
Date: January 18, 20xx
Manager:
Regarding employee: Bob Howland
Subject: Hiring practices

I am putting on record the decision by our in-house counsel to defend Mr. Howland and the organization from allegations of bias in hiring.

Mr. Howland has cooperated with the investigation by counsel. All records related to this allegation against Mr. Howland are being kept by the legal department.

Until this matter is resolved, we have directed Mr. Howland to involve a representative of the human resources department in all matters of hiring, firing, promotion, or discipline in his department.

PERFORMANCE EVALUATION: Acknowledging progress

Confidential: Personnel matter
Date: April 1, 20xx
Manager:
Regarding employee: Bob Howland
Subject: Hiring practices

An allegation of bias in hiring, lodged against Mr. Howland in January, has been dismissed by an arbitrator for lack of evidence. We appreciate Mr. Howland's cooperation with the legal department in this matter.

On the Wrong Side

Can an organization defend the continued employment of an admitted (or convicted) lawbreaker? That's not an easy question to answer.

Most organizations do try to give productive and well-meaning staffers every opportunity to correct mistakes and learn to get past problems. However, it is also true that keeping an employee who has been found to have violated a law may open the organization to greater liability from his or her own future actions or actions by others. (For example, if a plaintiff can demonstrate a history of discrimination in an organization and the fact that the source of the problem is still on the payroll, a judge or jury may be more inclined to believe a claim or to increase a penalty.)

That's the problem brought about by Johnny Skolnick. An employee in his department brought a lawsuit against the organization alleging that he passed her over for promotion because of her age. An arbiter ruled in her favor, and the organization was required to give her a promotion plus back pay. In addition, the organization was ordered to enter into a consent decree promising not to repeat the same sort of problem.

So, what about Johnny? Should he be fired? Should he be retrained? Should he be placed in a new position that does not include decision-making on hiring, firing, or promotions?

Some organizations will say that they do not want to expose themselves to future lawsuits or larger settlements by keeping such an employee on the payroll. Others might choose to remove someone like Johnny from a position in which he has any hiring or firing decision-making responsibilities.

Verbal Notification

I've asked you to meet with me today to discuss how we will deal with an allegation of age-based bias made by one of the staffers in your department. There may or may not be anything of concern here, but for legal reasons and the commitment of this organization to fair employment practices, we do take such matters seriously.

Because of the sensitive nature of this matter, do not go into details with me. I am directing you to immediately meet with the head of the human resources department.

MEMO TO FILE: Noting a request for action

Confidential: Personnel matter
Date: January 15, 20xx
Manager:
Regarding employee: Johnny Skolnick
Subject: Promotion practices

I met today with Mr. Skolnick to discuss dealing with an allegation of age-related bias made by a member of his department. I explained to him that there may or may not be anything of concern here, but for legal reasons and the commitment of this organization to fair employment practices, we do take such matters seriously.

I told him that because of the sensitive nature of this matter, I did not want him to go into detail with me. Instead, I asked him to immediately meet with the head of the human resources department.

Confidential: Personnel matter
Date: January 18, 20xx
Manager:
Regarding employee: Johnny Skolnick
Subject: Promotion practices

According to the human resources department, there has been no finding of any improper promotion practices by Mr. Skolnick.

They have requested, though, that he involve the human resources department in any hiring, firing, promotion, or discipline decision for the next year. I emphasized to Mr. Skolnick that this change in procedure was intended only to assist him in his management and was not intended as a punishment for any action.

Confidential: Personnel matter
Date: February 1, 20xx
Manager:
Regarding employee: Johnny Skolnick
Subject: Promotion practices

The human resources department has reported that Johnny Skolnick has fully cooperated with their request to be involved in all employment-related decision-making in his department.

Chapter 10

EXPERT OPINION: AN EMPLOYMENT LAWYER ON THE RECORD

ROBERT M. SHEA is a member in the law firm of Morse, Barnes-Brown & Pendleton, P.C., in Waltham, Massachusetts, where he counsels businesses and individuals in all areas of labor and employment law, including employment policies and practices, employment agreements, independent contractor relationships, discipline and discharge issues, Equal Employment Opportunity compliance, harassment training, claims and investigations, wage-hour compliance, leaves of absence, workplace privacy, employee drug-testing, non-competition, workforce reductions, and separation/severance agreements.

He regularly represents clients in employment discrimination, harassment, wrongful discharge, and wage-hour litigation before federal and state courts and agencies including the Equal Employment Opportunity Commission (EEOC) and the U.S. Department of Labor.

Mr. Shea lectures frequently on employment law issues and has written many articles for national and local publications. He is a former co-chair of the Boston Bar Association's labor and employment law section. He is also a mediator and arbitrator, and he serves on the American Arbitration Association's panel of employment arbitrators.

He graduated magna cum laude from Boston College in 1981 and received his J.D. with honors from George

Washington University National Law Center in 1984. He can be reached by e-mail at *rshea@mbbp.com*.

The interview that follows is not meant in any way as legal advice, and preceding chapters of this book represent the opinions and research of the authors and not the opinion of Mr. Shea. Please consult an appropriate attorney or human resources specialist for assistance on specific employment issues.

Q. *Putting aside things like personal employment contracts, collective bargaining agreements, and civil service regulations, and in the broadest of terms: What rights does an employer have when it comes to disciplining, reassigning, or firing an employee?*

A. In the broadest of terms, it is almost an absolute that you start with the presumption of at-will employment.

In forty-nine of the fifty states, employees are considered to be at will, meaning they can be terminated for good reason, bad reason, or no reason. With or without notice.

However, that right to terminate at will has changed over the years, so that statutory and common-law restrictions lead many employees to believe that any termination, any adverse action, needs to be supported by legitimate, nondiscriminatory business reasons.

But my view is that employers start with the absolute right to do what they need to do to promote the business interests of the company.

To my knowledge, Montana is the only state that has legislatively created a requirement of a cause for termination.

Q. *In what kind of situations are employers generally more limited in their ability to make decisions on employment status?*

A. There are collective bargaining agreements and individual employment contracts. And there are other types of contracts that may not be written but are oral promises.

I look at the restrictions on employers' conduct as moving from at-will to some sort of restriction in (these areas):

1. There are statutory restrictions. These are antidiscrimination laws that say you can't treat someone differently based on a protected category.
2. There are contractual restrictions, which include written contracts, oral promises, offer letters, and other statements or representations that cause an employee to have an expectation that there is some restriction on the employer's right to terminate.
3. Then there is the common law, where the courts have developed restrictions on the employer's right. You can't terminate someone in violation of public policy, for example. (One example of that is a whistleblower claim; someone alleges that they are being terminated because they complained about an unlawful practice by the employer.)
4. Many states impose a restriction against terminating someone to deprive them from receiving compensation that they have earned. (For example, a salesperson may be due a large commission on a sale. If the employer terminates that person, argu-

ably that commission has been earned and is owed to the employee.)

Q. *There are also situations that bar employers from terminating a worker just before a pension or other economic program is about to become available.*

A. With a pension it would be a statutory restriction such as the Employee Retirement Income Security Act (ERISA), which prohibits an employer from terminating someone to deprive them from monies owed under a plan regulated by ERISA.

If it is a stock option plan, it may fall into what's called a breach of covenant or good faith, depriving someone of money that has been earned and owed to them.

Q. *Again, in the broadest terms, what are acceptable reasons for terminating, disciplining, or reassigning an employee?*

A. Performance, misconduct, or change in economic circumstances: Those are three of the most common acceptable reasons.

It would not be unlawful to terminate someone because you don't like their personality or because your brother-in-law wants that position.

But when you go beyond performance, misconduct, or the economic or financial needs of the company to factors such as personal like or dislike, or some sort of allegiance to someone based on friendship or family, then it becomes easier for an employee to challenge that termination or demotion or a poor performance review as discriminatory or retaliatory.

Part of showing that you have been discriminated against or treated unlawfully is to show that the reason given by the employer is untrue. Someone says: "I believe I was chosen for termination because I am older. I am sixty-two years old, and my manager is thirty-five, and I believe my manager is favoring younger employees."

If the sixty-two-year-old is terminated or receives a demotion or a very critical performance review, the employer should support [that action] with either poor performance or misconduct or some legitimate economic or financial reason, which could include salary considerations.

The employer is not going to want to support it with something like, "I don't like his personality," or, "His replacement is a good friend of mine," because it doesn't look right. It doesn't look fair.

If someone claims discrimination, the fact finder may be a jury, it may be a judge, or it may be some administrative agency. There is going to be an expectation that the employer acted reasonably, for "acceptable" reasons such as performance, misconduct, or financial concerns of the company.

Q. *Is it lawful for an employer to say, "We were forced to lay off this sixty-two-year-old man or woman who is earning $100,000 and instead hire a kid out of college for $30,000 per year?"*

A. Generally speaking, it is lawful to do that.

But when there is a correlation between age and income, as there frequently is, the employer is certainly open to a challenge that this is an attempt to get rid of older workers [rather than a financial decision].

Q. *Realizing that someone can file suit over almost anything, whether or not they have a valid claim, what is the best course of action that an employer should take to try to avoid lawsuits?*

A. Be truthful, be fair, and have your actions appear to be fair to the outside world.

In terms of what employers do wrong, I think they frequently get themselves in trouble because they are not as candid or frank as they should be. Sometimes [they do this] to spare the feelings of the employee.

[Sometimes employers get into trouble trying] to hide some other motivation that may or may not be unlawful. But most commonly it is because they have a difficult time presenting the bad news, so they use terms like, "We are laying you off" when "layoff" may imply that there is some reduction in force for economic reasons and not performance reasons.

Generally, our advice is to be truthful in an empathetic but direct way. One of the ways that employees are able to establish discrimination or unlawful retaliation is by disproving the reason given by the employer. So, when an employer tries to spare the employee's feelings, giving a reason that is not quite the truth, they get locked into that reason.

If the employee challenges that dismissal later on, claiming discrimination, the employer has difficulty separating themselves from the reason the employer gave at the time of termination.

[Without] direct evidence of discrimination [through statements like], "We are getting rid of you because we think you are a dinosaur," or, "You can't teach an old dog new tricks," or, "You are just getting too old," the key for an employee [filing suit] is to show that the reasons given by the employer are untrue.

And so, rule number one is: Be truthful. We tell clients, don't beat the employee over the head with their failures, but whatever you tell the employee, make sure it is truthful. Be fair, and do it in a setting that doesn't unnecessarily embarrass the employee.

Offer appropriate support to the employee where possible. It could be outplacement services. It could be discussions about references. It could be assurances about the company's position with respect to unemployment compensation. But do so in a way to the extent possible that the employee is able to keep [his or her] dignity and believe that the employer is treating them as fairly as possible.

Q. *One source of problems for employers arises out of the employee evaluation itself. There is a tendency by some managers to try to be nice or at least neutral in what they put in writing. And then they have to turn around and answer to the employee or to a court or arbitrator why someone who has a history of good evaluations has been dismissed because of poor performance.*

A. Far too many times we are asked to defend a lawsuit in which an employee was terminated for poor performance, and we are told at the outset it is well documented that the performance evaluations reflect the deficiencies. Then we look at those evaluations as we begin our defense of the case and see a completely different story.

There are evaluations where the difference is modest or marginal. The terminated employee [may have] received "good" or "very good" [ratings], and the other people in the group received "excellents" or "outstandings."

It becomes difficult when you have to explain to a fact finder, judge, jury, or agency that "very good" wasn't good enough. [Or you have to show how] that employee fit in with respect to the other employees who were not terminated.

[It would be helpful if you] can establish a timeline because when a current employee is filing a lawsuit or threatening to file a lawsuit, it really takes the risk to a different level. You are not just talking about discrimination then; you are talking about potential [claims of] retaliation. I would say that in the last ten years, retaliation complaints have increased dramatically while discrimination cases have stayed fairly steady.

I think to some extent lawyers who represent employees have come to realize that retaliation claims are easier to prove. And they tend to be more lucrative because juries and judges don't like retaliation against someone exercising their rights. They tend to punish the employer in the form of punitive damages when the employer has not taken the steps to protect the employee from unlawful retaliation.

In my view, it is easier to establish retaliation than proving that someone was treated differently, terminated, or treated more harshly because of their race, as an example. You basically have to establish that the manager involved is racist, in some way.

Proving retaliation is much easier because it is human nature to want to strike back at someone who is hurting you or accusing you of bad conduct. I think that resonates with a jury when they are evaluating a set of facts. It is much easier for them to believe that a manager didn't like the fact that an employee was bringing a charge of discrimination. It is very easy for the jury to believe that a manager started considering that in making employment decisions.

And so, back to your question about what should an employer do when an employee raises the L word: *lawsuit*. Our general advice is to proceed to be able to show that your actions and your subsequent treatment of the employee—including things like a sixty-day-review period and steps the employee needs to achieve—are proceeding in the same way they would if the employee never raised the L word.

Q. *At what point should a manager say, "This has risen to the level where I need to get our counsel involved before I do anything"?*

A. Immediately. For some organizations, the first stop may be the human resources department. Managers should be trained that whenever legal issues, or any is-

264

sues that concern interpretation of policy arise, human resources should be contacted.

And I think human resources should be trained to contact outside counsel or in-house counsel whenever the specter of a legal claim is raised because you are immediately into a higher level of risk because of the possibility of a claim of retaliation.

Q. *What is the proper way to handle an employee who you suspect is violating a criminal or civil law?*

A. In general, I don't think you should make accusations concerning an employee, particularly when it involves criminal activity, without having performed some sort of investigation first. The biggest area of danger for employers in this situation is defamation claims.

Focus on the facts, not making a statement of conclusion or accusation but rather looking for an explanation of something that has come to the employer's attention.

Q. *So you might say: "We have three ticket windows all selling the same product and each having the same number of opportunities. And yet your results are 30 percent below the windows to the left and right. Can you tell me why this might be case?"*

A. Exactly. That's a fair question.

Q. *And then what do you do if the employee says, "One of my children has a health problem, and I took several thousand* *dollars out of the cash drawer, and I feel terrible about it. I will never do it again"?*

A. If it is in fact a serious violation that may lead to a discipline including termination or may lead to some sort of a criminal prosecution, I would get legal involved.

I would sit and listen. I wouldn't take any action or make any representation. There may need to be further investigation and an evaluation of employer's responsibilities and obligations. There could be customers and other third parties involved.

There should be concerns about [the possibility of a defamation claim as the result of] drawing conclusions too quickly and accusing the person of a crime.

But you are getting information here, and this might be the only or the best opportunity to get this employee's explanation, because after the meeting the employee may decide that their interests are better served by talking to a lawyer or just keeping their mouth shut.

But the employee has raised the issue. They are telling you their explanation. There might be some personal reasons.

My view is "Be all ears." Listen to their explanation.

I don't see why you wouldn't take notes. That would be the normal practice here. If you are having a meeting with an employee like this, you would either take notes or you would be preparing a memo to the file or some sort of documentation of the meeting.

If you need notes to make sure you have an accurate record of the meeting, then you should take notes.

Q. *One big concern for many organizations is an allegation of sexual harassment. Let's talk about a situation that has not risen to the level of a complaint. What are the first steps to take when you become aware of a potential problem?*

A. I would hope that the employer has a policy in place that at least provides some guidance to human resources, managers, and above on how to react to a complaint.

But a rule of thumb would be: Take any complaint seriously, and be very liberal in how you view any complaints that you believe might fall into the category of harassment, sexual, racial, or other kinds.

Is someone guilty until proven innocent? Absolutely not.

And we know in harassment situations, particularly in sexual harassment situations, there can be a lot of gray areas. There could be complaints made for ulterior motives.

Q. *Let's talk about those gray areas.*

A. Some people claim harassment where it is not really sexual but (instead) just harsh criticism of their performance or a demanding supervisor.

[A company policy] would likely tell a manager to contact human resources [and that would lead to] an investigation by either human resources or legal.

The rights of the alleged harassed employee, as well as the alleged harasser, are important.

Q. *There are no laws that say a manager cannot date someone he or she supervises, correct? At the same time, there are* *no laws that say an organization cannot have a policy that bans such a relationship.*

A. You are right on both scores. There is no law that prohibits a supervisor from dating a subordinate, but it's usually not a good practice. It is certainly fraught with danger.

If the relationship turns sour, the subordinate [could] claim that [he or she is] being treated differently based on the relationship. Or [there could be claims] from other employees of the same or different gender claiming that they are treated less favorably than the subordinate who is having a relationship with the superior.

Can employers prohibit it? Yes, generally speaking, although there are some instances where it could have an adverse impact on one gender or the other. A no-dating policy has to be looked at very carefully; some companies have interim steps.

Q. *Other areas of concern for employers include allegations of retaliation against whistleblowers or actions taken against employees who report possible civil violations to state or federal agencies on their own.*

A. An employer should anticipate that possibility and [have in place] a policy that protects employees from retaliation with respect to other ways in which they might exercise their legal rights.

If there is an allegation of retaliation, involve the human resources department. Be proactive. You may end up making a transfer of the employee or the managers or inserting another person in the reporting relationship or the performance evaluation relationship . . . to ensure that there is no unlawful retaliation taking place.

If there is a complaint of retaliation, it should be investigated. And that may mean looking at prior evaluations [and comparing them] to subsequent evaluations or the evaluation that the employee claims is the result of retaliation.

Q. *As a manager who prepares memos to file or performance evaluations, should you make note of a suspicion of wrongdoing or an unproven accusation? Are there some things that should not be put down in writing?*

A. Generally, yes. A memo to file [should be] focused on facts or performance problems or what occurred in a meeting. Just the facts.

Managers get in trouble when they start drawing conclusions and putting [them] in their memos to file. These conclusions may be based on speculation or conjecture. Unfortunately, we see some memos to file that include references to employees' personal issues or health issues.

This is generally not a good idea because they might be wrong, or they could be creating evidence that might be used to support a disability discrimination case.

If you are writing a memo about a meeting, it should be about what was said at the meeting. If you are writing a memo about performance problems, it should be about the performance problems.

[The memo should state] what the manager has seen, or where the employee has failed to perform, and not draw conclusions about the person's personality, family issues, or health issues.

Q. *On the other hand, what if an employee volunteers information to a manager? What if the employee says something like, "The reason I have not been very productive or the reason I have been lashing out at others in the office is that I am going through a divorce." Is that the sort of thing that could properly be included in a memo to file?*

A. If the purpose of the memo is to document a meeting, then an employee's explanation for their performance problems would be appropriate to include in the memo. You are documenting the communication.

The memo may be something like this: "On Thursday, February 1, I met with John Jones to discuss his performance. I said this. John Jones said that." It is a report on a meeting.

If this is really a discussion regarding a performance review, and we are talking about performance problems and ways in which the employee can improve those problems, then talking about their divorce or about other personal issues probably should not be included in the performance evaluation.

Once you start addressing personal or health issues, you have to be very careful.

Q. *Is there any situation as a manager in which you should say to an employee, "Stop. You should not be telling me this"?*

A. If an employee is explaining something and providing personal information, I don't think there is a legal obligation on the part of the employer to say, "stop."

The problem [would be if] the employer follows up with additional questions or draws out the information with questions.

I don't think the employer has to say, "stop," but once the employer or the manager hears these things, it puts the employer on notice concerning some of these issues. If an employee is explaining their performance problems by saying, "I am undergoing some treatment for a particular condition," a manager can't just ignore that.

That notice to the manager becomes notice to the employer, and it may trigger obligations to provide reasonable accommodation to the employee. [The employer may be obliged] to engage in what the EEOC calls an interactive process for determining what reasonable accommodation can be provided.

Sometimes it becomes evident that the employee needs a flexible schedule. It may mean [the employer will have to] cut a little more slack in their performance targets.

Some managers and employers prefer to have their head in the sand and not hear these things because it puts them on notice. But it is difficult if the employee, without any particular prompting, says these things. The employer can't be in the position of saying, "I don't want to hear about your health issues. I just want you to do the job."

If the employee puts it on the table, it often triggers some obligation on the part of the employer.

Q. *You have said that, in general, it would not be proper to ask an underperforming employee if he or she is having health or family issues. Can you ask a more general question, like, "Is there a reason you would like to share with me about why your performance has fallen off in recent weeks?"*

A. I think that's a fair question. It may be, "Why has your performance fallen off 50 percent? What's causing it? What can we do to turn it around?"

Coming from my employment lawyer perspective, it may be unrealistic, but I am concerned that what the employer says can be twisted around or mischaracterized later on by employees.

By saying, "Is there anything you need to share with me?" it may be turned around later on to say, "My manager was looking to find out if I had any health issues or if I had any personal issues."

Q. *But it doesn't always work to just stick to the facts: "Last month you made 1,000 widgets and this month only 500."*

A. Right. We are dealing with humans. There are relationships and friendships and genuine concern. You can't expect managers and employees to be robots.

So, expressions of concern regarding someone's personal or physical well-being is natural. And where it is obvious to an employer—someone walking with a limp or a sudden loss in weight—when it is clear that there is something going on from a health standpoint, then I think it becomes a little bit more acceptable to make some inquiry.

But as a result of the Americans with Disability Act, HIPAA [the Health Insurance Portability and Accountability Act of 1996, which includes safeguards for the privacy of medical records], and other restrictions concerning privacy employers have to be very careful.

Q. *Let's talk about arrests and other legal problems that take place away from the workplace. In general, is the employer allowed to inquire about these matters or to insist upon notification?*

A. Generally speaking, I think the employer would be overstepping [to inquire] about conduct or crimes that are unrelated to an employee's position or their ability to perform their jobs.

But certainly there are employment agreements that have morals clauses, and sometimes commission of a felony would be cause for termination. You might be the comptroller, the CFO, or accounts receivable person where you have access to the funds of the company, and a crime that involves fraud or embezzlement might call into question your ability or your trustworthiness to perform your job.

Q. *So if an organization has a specific reason to require disclosure—insurance bonding or governmental regulations—there are situations where an employer can insist on notification.*

A. Yes. But this raises the whole issue of privacy, which is almost by definition a gray area. When does the business interest of the company outweigh the privacy interests of the employer? It is hard to pinpoint.

There are some situations where the employer has notified employees about how it views privacy. For example, if the employer tells employees through a clearly communicated policy that if you use our computer system and our e-mail system, you shouldn't have any expectation of privacy.

Similarly, a locker, a desk, an office: If you make it clear to employees that it is company property and you don't have an expectation of privacy, it is much easier for an employer later on to look at employees' e-mails or to search an employee's locker or desk.

Again, if we are starting with the assumption that a worker is employed at-will and could be terminated for any reason, I was expressing my view that most employers are willing to distinguish between personal activity and job-related activity.

It doesn't mean that they legally are obligated to make that distinction. If someone is an at-will employee, and the employer doesn't like the fact that he or she was involved in a bar fight and was arrested, and they decide to terminate the employee for that reason, they are free to do so, generally speaking.

And if a bus company has a rule or a practice that they terminate someone if they learn that a bus driver has traffic infractions even outside their job, I don't believe that is unlawful. I believe it is within the employer's prerogative to take that action.

Where employers may get in trouble is to what extent they are looking into private information. Are they invading privacy rights of employees?

Let's face it, though: With particular occupations like truck drivers, school bus drivers, airline pilots, teachers, positions that involve public safety, there is going to be a high tolerance for employers having higher standards.

That's where the balance between business interests and employee privacy rights would weigh more on behalf of the employer and against the employee.

Q. *In general, what does the law say about an employer's ability to compel overtime?*

A. Generally, employers are free to compel overtime. There are certain restrictions with respect to breaks and the payment of overtime pay. And requiring exempt employees to work sixty or seventy hours a week without being paid overtime is generally not unlawful.

Requiring non-exempt employees, salaried or hourly, to work those hours and paying them time and a half is also not unlawful. There are Blue Law restrictions concerning holidays and Sundays in some states, but otherwise compelling employees to work longer hours even if it means over forty hours a week is lawful.

Q. *Are there any protected classes when it comes to overtime? Can an employee refuse overtime because he or she needs to be home to provide child care, for example?*

A. That's a good question. There are exceptions in some areas. Certainly, people who have disabilities or health conditions may receive a reasonable accommodation, which might mean a reduced work schedule.

As far as child care, this is an evolving area. I do not think most states prohibit employers from requiring all employees who do not have a serious health condition or disability to work the hours the employer demands, even if they have child care issues.

I think we are going to see for a while some inconsistent decisions on the rights of working mothers and fathers and what employers can require in terms of their commitment to the job. I think perhaps in some future legislation on the issue you are going to see courts pigeonhole those types of claims into existing laws prohibiting gender discrimination or those that allow family and medical leave.

If you believe a lot of the doomsayers we are going to have an employee shortage, and employers will fight over a decreasing pool of educated workers.

Many employers will end up being motivated more by those considerations than by the legal requirements. Market conditions are driving employer behavior.

Q. *Is there a generally accepted standard that defines a "trial period" for new employees during which the worker can be dismissed for any reason?*

A. I think it is really more an issue of expectations. If you are starting with the assumption that employees are employed at-will, then you could fire someone on day two or day ninety-two.

But there is an expectation among employees that they are going to be given an opportunity to prove themselves. An employee may have left a job to join a new employer, and perhaps have moved, so there is an expectation that they are going to be given some period before they might be terminated for poor performance.

In some jobs, a trial period of ninety days or six months is explicit. It may be a job where it is going to be known within a relatively short time whether someone is going to make it or not.

Q. *How far does an employer have to go when it comes to making accommodations for a worker with special needs?*

A. First of all there is the concept of just being fair and loyal to employees, doing the right thing. And then there are the legal requirements.

When it comes to the law, there are the requirements imposed by the federal Family and Medical Leave Act for employers of fifty or more and similar requirements under state laws.

And then there are disability discrimination laws, at the federal level and in most states, which say generally speaking if someone has a mental or physical impairment that substantially limits a major life activity, but they are still able to perform the essential functions of the job either with or without a reasonable accommodation, then they are protected, and the employer cannot discriminate against them. The employer has to provide reasonable accommodation, if that is necessary, to allow them to perform the essential functions of the job.

From an employer's perspective, when an employee meets the definitions [of the law], they have to provide reasonable accommodation. This may include allowing them to have a leave of absence, taking away certain non-essential job functions, putting them on a flexible work schedule, or reducing their work hours.

Q. *There obviously are some situations where an accommodation cannot be reached. The classic examples are usually things like an airline pilot or a truck driver who loses his sight.*

A. I think that is a clear-cut example of where the employer can draw the line. Where an employee cannot perform the essential function of the job—if it is a truck driver job, and the person can no longer drive a truck—the employer can choose to terminate employment. They can offer whatever benefits the employee has under a short-term disability or long-term disability policy, but not to continue employment.

INDEX

ABOUT THE AUTHORS

Corey Sandler is author of more than one hundred books on business, computers, travel, and other topics. Earlier in his career he worked as an executive for newspaper and magazine companies, managing staffs of more than a hundred. He also held a job as a mid-level manager for an agency of New York state government and an administrative post for a major university.

Janice Keefe is a researcher and author of business books. She has worked for several publishing companies as well as a state agency.

Among their bestselling books on business are *Performance Appraisals That Work* and *Performance Appraisal Phrase Book*. You can learn more about the authors and contact them through their Web site, *www.econoguide.com*.

Printed in the United States
By Bookmasters